CONTRARY

● to Popular Belief ●

**More than
250
False Facts
Revealed**

CONTRARY

to Popular Belief

More than
250
False Facts
Revealed

Joey Green

Broadway Books / New York

Let us begin by committing ourselves to the truth;

to see it like it is and tell it like it is;

to find the truth, to speak the truth, and to live the truth.

—*Richard M. Nixon*
Nomination acceptance speech
at the Republican Convention,
August 8, 1968

INTRODUCTION

The Declaration of Independence was signed on August 2, 1776. In *The Wizard of Oz*, Dorothy wears silver shoes. Giovanni da Verrazano discovered the Hudson River. Panama hats come from Ecuador. Alaska is the easternmost state in the United States. In the Bible, Moses climbs up Mount Sinai seven times. The Earth is closest to the Sun on January 1.

Sounds like a pack of lies, doesn't it? Remarkably, they're all facts—accurate, indisputable, and verifiably true.

Impossible, you say? The truth is: we've all come to accept a bunch of fallacies, falsehoods, and hearsay as genuine truth. We rarely demand substantiation. We're either too trusting or too lazy to run to the library to look it up.

And so, as a public service, I locked myself away in the library, checking and double-checking the facts, determined to expose the hundreds of myths we've believed unsuspectingly, the misconceptions we've retold to others, and the unmitigated balderdash that has poisoned our collective consciousness. Here, then, is the antidote. It's empowering, liberating, and guaranteed to set you free. It's called the truth. Please use it wisely.

{ **George Washington was the ninth
president of the United States.** }

The United States was established on July 4, 1776. George Washington was inaugurated president thirteen years later, on April 30, 1789. During the intervening years, the Second Continental Congress in Philadelphia drew up the Articles of Confederation (the first American constitution). In 1781, Maryland representative John Hanson was elected the first president of the Congress of the Confederation. His official title was "president of the United States in Congress Assembled." After Hanson, seven other men served as president: Elias Boudinot, Thomas Mifflin, Richard Henry Lee, John Hancock, Nathaniel Gorham, Arthur St. Clair, and Cyrus Griffin. In 1787, Congress held a constitutional convention. The delegates wrote the current constitution, ratified by the states in 1788. The following year, the ratifying states elected Washington our nation's ninth president (but the first president under the new constitution).

The song "As Time Goes By" was not written for the movie *Casablanca*.

"As Time Goes By" (music by Herman Hupfeld, lyrics by Irving Kahal) was originally sung in the 1931 Broadway stage show *Everybody's Welcome*, and Rudy Vallee recorded the song later that year. *Casablanca* premiered eleven years later in 1942. The popularity of the movie prompted RCA to rerelease the Rudy Vallee recording.

{ The Black Hills of South Dakota are not hills. }

Hills rise less than 1,000 feet from the surrounding area, while mountains rise above that height. The Black Hills rise from 2,000 to 4,000 feet above the surrounding area. Several peaks exceed 6,000 feet, and the highest "hill," Harney Peak, reaches 7,242 feet, higher than any peak in the Appalachian or Ozark mountains. The Sioux Indians named the mountains Paha Sapa ("hills of black") because from the plains, the pine trees covering the mountains appear black (and because the Sioux had no idea geologists strictly distinguished between hills and mountains).

{ **The Earl of Sandwich did not invent the sandwich.** }

History's first recorded sandwich is the Hillel sandwich, invented by Rabbi Hillel between 70 B.C.E and 10 C.E. The sandwich, eaten during Passover seders, consists of charosets (a combination of fruits, nuts, and honey) and bitter herbs between two pieces of *matzah* (Hebrew for "unleavened bread"). As early as the Middle Ages, Arabs have eaten meat stuffed inside a pocket of pita bread, and medieval European peasants ate bread and cheese lunches in the fields. John Montagu, the fourth Earl of Sandwich (1718–1792), did eat sliced meats and cheeses between two pieces of bread to keep one hand free while playing cards at the gambling table, giving the sandwich its name, but not its origin.

The tuxedo did not originate in England.

In the summer of 1886, Pierre Lorillard IV, living in Tuxedo Park, a small hamlet in Westchester County, New York, did not want to wear formal black tie and tails to the annual Autumn Ball at his country club. He commissioned a tailor to make several semiformal tailless black jackets—in the style of the scarlet riding jackets popular with British fox hunters. Black tie and tails originated in England in the early 1800s. Lorillard may have been inspired by Edward VII, who during a visit to India as Prince of Wales had ordered the tails cut off his coat to keep cool in the heat. Ultimately, Lorillard did not wear the new dinner jacket to the ball, but his son, Griswold, and some of Griswold's friends, did—starting a trend. The jacket became known as the tuxedo, after the town, which was named after Algonquin Indian chief P'tauk-Seet (the *P* is silent), meaning "wolf."

{ Congress did not sign the Declaration of Independence on July 4, 1776. }

On July 4, 1776, the Second Continental Congress, meeting in Philadelphia at the Pennsylvania State House, formally adopted the final draft of the Declaration of Independence. Only John Hancock, as president of Congress, and Charles Thomson, congressional secretary, signed it. The State of New York did not vote on it until July 9. On July 15, Congress ordered that the declaration be written on parchment, and on August 2, fifty assembled delegates signed the final document. Six others signed the document on later dates, including some who were not members of Congress when the declaration was adopted and Thomas McKean, who signed his name five years later, in 1781.

In June 1815, Britain's Duke of Wellington led troops
against Napoleon and his troops in a small valley four
miles to the south of Waterloo in Belgium between
the villages of Plancenoit and Mont St. Jean. The
battle became known as Waterloo possibly because
Wellington slept in Waterloo the night before, or because after the victory, he returned to Waterloo to
write home with the news.

Camels do not carry water in their humps.

Camels do not have a reservoir for liquids in their hump. The hump is a food reserve made primarily of fat. By storing most of its body fat in the hump, the camel can lose heat freely from the rest of its body without having to perspire much, thereby conserving water. A camel can go for days or even months without water because, unlike other animals, camels retain urea and do not start sweating until their body temperatures reach 115 degrees Fahrenheit.

The most abused drug is not alcohol.

The most abused drug in the world is caffeine—found in sodas, coffee, tea, cocoa, chocolate candies, and many over-the-counter medicines. According to the National Institute on Drug Abuse, caffeine is an addictive drug that creates physical dependence and causes an increase in heart rate, body temperature, urine production, and gastric juice secretion. Caffeine can also raise blood sugar levels and cause tremors, loss of coordination, decreased appetite, and postponement of fatigue, and it can interfere with the depth of sleep and the amount of dream sleep.

Paul Revere did not single-handedly make a midnight ride to warn American colonists that the British were coming.

Paul Revere was one of three riders on the famous midnight ride of April 18, 1775, from Boston to Concord, Massachusetts. The other two were William Dawes and Samuel Prescott. In the poem "Paul Revere's Ride" by Henry Wadsworth Longfellow, only Revere rides to Concord, after seeing one lantern light in the steeple of the Old North Church. In reality, the signal was not sent to Revere. He had directed that the signal be sent to friends in Charlestown. The "midnight ride" began at 1 A.M., and along the way Revere, Dawes, and Prescott ran into a British cavalry patrol. Dawes and Prescott escaped, but Revere was captured, detained, and forced to walk back to Lexington without his horse. Dawes also returned to Lexington. Only Prescott made it to Concord.

The potato did not originate in Ireland.

As early as 200 C.E., the Incas cultivated the potato in the Andes Mountains in what is now Peru and Bolivia. In the sixteenth century, Spanish conquistadors brought the potato to Europe. Soon after, English explorers brought potatoes to England. From there, potatoes were introduced to Ireland, where Irish farmers began growing them. The horrors of the Irish potato famine of the late 1840s, during which some 750,000 Irish people starved to death, cause people to wrongly conclude that the potato originated in Ireland. A statue of Sir Francis Drake in Offenbach, Germany, wrongly proclaims the English explorer as "Introducer of the Potato into Europe." There is no evidence that Drake, who sailed around South America, carried potatoes aboard his ship, the *Pelican*.

The Earth is not a sphere.

The Earth, flattened at the poles and bulging at the equator, is actually an oblate spheroid. In other words, the distance around the Earth along the equator (24,901.55 miles) is greater than the distance around the Earth through the North and South poles (24,859.82 miles). According to Sir Isaac Newton, this bulge is caused by the rotating Earth's centrifugal force.

Alaska is not only the westernmost state, but also the easternmost state. Some of Alaska's Aleutian Islands (the Rat Islands and the Near Islands) lie west of the 180th meridian, the dividing line between the Eastern Hemisphere and the Western Hemisphere, placing them securely in the Eastern Hemisphere.

Chess did not originate in Russia.

Chess began in sixth-century India as a game called *chaturanga* ("army" in Sanskrit) using miniature chariots, cavalry, infantry, and elephants as playing pieces. The game spread to Persia, which was conquered by the Arabs in the seventh century. Arab invaders brought the game to Spain in the tenth century, where it spread throughout Europe. The Europeans gradually changed the playing pieces to bishops, knights, pawns, and rooks. The Arabs had renamed the game *al-schah-mat* ("the king is dead" in Arabic), which in English became the word *checkmate*. In Russia, chess is called *schahkmat*. The English word *chess* comes from the Persian word *shah*, meaning "king." People think chess originated in Russia because Russians held the official world chess championship title from 1948 until 1972, when American Bobby Fisher beat Boris Spassky. The Russians regained the title in 1975 and held it through 2004.

{ Jesus was not born on December 25, 1 A.D. }

Nobody knows when Jesus when born. The New Testament does not specify the date. In the third century C.E., church father Clement of Alexandria suggested May 20, since the New Testament states that the shepherds who were told by an angel of Jesus's birth were watching their flocks during the night (Luke 2:9), which was done only in the spring at lambing time. In 336 C.E., the Western Church decided to celebrate December 25 as Jesus's birthday (officially adopted by Bishop Liberius of Rome in 354 C.E.), to usurp the popular Roman pagan feast of Natalis Solis Invicti ("birthday of the unconquerable sun"), honoring the Persian sun god Mithras. For centuries, pagans had celebrated the death and resurrection of the sun on the winter solstice in late December, and around 274 C.E., Roman emperor Aurelian had proclaimed Mithraism the official state religion.

The Eastern Orthodox Church and the Ukrainian Catholic Church still follow the Julian calendar, established by Julius Caesar in 45 B.C.E., celebrating Jesus's birthday on January 6.

In the sixth century C.E., a monk, Dionysius Exiguus, began counting the years from the year of Jesus's birth, which he miscalculated to be four to eight years later than the actual date. Since Jesus was born during the lifetime of Herod the Great, his birth had to take place before Herod's death in 4 B.C.E.

The New Testament states that Caesar Augustus ordered a census, compelling Joseph to bring his pregnant wife, Mary, to Bethlehem. Ancient documents seem to indicate that a census took place between 6 and 8 B.C.E.

So, while most Christians celebrate the birth of Jesus on December 25, Jesus was more likely born in the spring—sometime between 4 and 8 B.C.E.

Ferdinand Magellan was not the first explorer to sail around the world.

Magellan, a Portuguese seaman whose real name was Fernão de Magalhães, led an expedition of five ships from Spain in 1519, navigated what would become known as the Strait of Magellan at the southern tip of South America, became the first European to sail the Pacific, and discovered Guam and the Philippines, where the indigenous people killed him on the island of Mactan in 1521. One of Magellan's officers, Juan Sebastián del Cano, led one ship back to Spain in 1522, completing the first circumnavigation of the world. The first explorer to sail around the world was Sir Francis Drake.

The seventeeth president of the United States was not Ulysses S. Grant.

His parents named him Hiram Ulysses Grant, but they called him Ulysses. In 1839, the congressman who appointed Ulysses to the

U.S. Military Academy at West Point mistakenly reported the youth's name to the registrar as Ulysses S. Grant. He thought Ulysses was the young man's first name and his middle name that of his mother's family, Simpson. Grant, convinced that his classmates might tease him over his real initials (H.U.G.), never corrected the mistake.

Benjamin Franklin did not found the *Saturday Evening Post.*

In 1899, editor George Horace Lorimer started running the phrase "Founded A.D. 1728 by Benjamin Franklin" on the cover of the

Saturday Evening Post to sell more magazines. The *Saturday Evening Post* actually had been founded in 1821, thirty-one years after Benjamin Franklin's death. In 1729, Franklin did buy and operate the *Pennsylvania Gazette*, a small newspaper that continued publishing after his death in 1790, finally going defunct in 1815, six years before the first issue of the *Saturday Evening Post* hit the press—in the same print shop where the *Pennsylvania Gazette* had been printed.

{ James Watt did not invent the steam engine. }

In 1698, Thomas Savery patented the first practical steam engine, a pump used to drain flooded mines in Cornwall, England. Steam entered a sealed vessel through a hand-operated valve, cold water was poured on the vessel to condense the steam inside and create a partial vacuum, then the valve was opened so the vacuum could suck water up a pipe and into the vessel. In 1712, English blacksmith Thomas Newcomen invented a steam engine that powered a piston. In 1763, Scottish engineer James Watt improved on a Newcomen engine by introducing the idea of two separate chambers for vaporization and condensation, rather than one chamber, which wasted enormous amounts of steam. He received a patent for his innovation in 1769, but to say that Watt invented the steam engine is nothing but a lot of hot air.

Adolf Hitler did not paint houses or hang wallpaper.

After failing the entrance examination to the Academy of Fine Arts in Vienna, Austria, two years in a row, Adolf Hitler supported himself by making posters for shopkeepers and by painting picture postcards that he peddled in taverns. He did take odd jobs shoveling snow, carrying suitcases at the Vienna train station, and as a day laborer on construction projects, but he never made a living painting houses or hanging wallpaper. However, on October 4, 1939, one month after Hitler invaded Poland, the French weekly *Marianne* published on its front page a satirical photo montage—created by Danish photographer Jacob "Marinus" Kjeldgaard—depicting Hitler as a housepainter. Soon afterward, the French air-dropped 200,000 postcards of the image over Germany. The image also appeared in an estimated 140 American newspapers and magazines.

The world's largest pyramid is not in Egypt.

The Quetzalcóatl, the largest pyramid in the world, sits in Cholula de Rivadabia, sixty-three miles southeast of Mexico City. Built between the second and sixth centuries C.E. and dedicated to the Aztec god Quetzalcóatl, the pyramid rises 177 feet and covers nearly 45 acres. By comparison, Egypt's Great Pyramid of Cheops, built in the third millennium B.C.E., rises just 130 feet and covers less than 13 acres—but clearly gets much better publicity.

Quetzalcóatl

Great Pyramid of Cheops

The song "Yankee Doodle" was not written by American colonists during the Revolutionary War.

Most historians believe that a dapper British soldier, Dr. Richard Shuckburg, wrote the song in 1755 during the French and Indian Wars, to ridicule American colonial militiamen's motley clothes, outdated equipment, and lack of military training. A Yankee Doodle is a ragamuffin country bumpkin from New England who sticks a feather in his cap to be stylish, but actually looks ridiculous. British soldiers sang the ditty to demoralize the colonists as they marched to the Battle of Concord. When the colonists won the battle, they sang the derisive song as their own defiant patriotic cheer. So stick a feather in that!

The name *Smith* is not short for "blacksmith."

Surnames are usually based on a place of residence, an ancestor's given name, or an occupation—such as Baker, Carpenter, Cook, Miller, and Taylor. The most common surname in the English language is Smith. A smith is a person who works with metal. The word *smith* originated before the word *blacksmith*. A blacksmith is actually a type of smith who works with iron. A whitesmith works with tin.

The island of Atlantis did not sink into the ocean.

The story of the island of Atlantis sinking into the ocean originated in Plato's dialogue *Timaeus*, written around 350 B.C.E. Plato fancifully described Atlantis as the beautiful and prosperous home to an empire that once dominated parts of Europe and Africa. The impiety of the people causes earthquakes and floods, and the sea swallows up the island. There is no mention of any such island in the writings of any other author before Plato. The Greek philosopher's most famous student, Aristotle, said only one thing about Atlantis: "He who invented it also destroyed it." Some scientists believe Plato based his fictitious tale on the volcanic eruption that destroyed the island of Thira, in the Aegean Sea, around 1500 B.C.E.

Julius Caesar was not the first emperor of Rome.

Roman general and statesman Julius Caesar, who ruled Rome as a monarch without a crown, died on March 15, 44 B.C.E., thirteen years before Rome become an empire in 31 B.C.E. Not until 29 B.C.E. did the Roman senate make Julius Caesar's grandnephew, Octavian (who had defeated Antony and Cleopatra in the Battle of

Actium) the first emperor of Rome. Octavian took the name Caesar Augustus. The next four emperors also used the name Caesar, which eventually became synonymous with the title *emperor.*

The sinking of the American ship *Lusitania* did not prompt the United States to enter World War I.

A German U-boat torpedoed and sank the *Lusitania*, a British passenger ship traveling through a declared war zone, on May 7, 1915—two years before the United States entered World War I. On the day the *Lusitania* had left America for Europe, advertisements placed by German officials living in the United States ran in fifty newspapers warning Americans not to travel on British ships carrying munitions. Despite the warnings, nearly 200 Americans boarded the *Lusitania*, which was transporting Canadian troops and 4,200 cases of rifle cartridges. Of the 1,924 people aboard, 1,198 died, including 128 Americans. The *Lusitania* became a rallying cry for Americans wishing to declare war against Germany. In response, Germany ordered its submarine commanders not to attack unarmed passenger ships. In 1917, Germany reversed its policy and announced unrestricted submarine warfare, prompting the United States to enter the war on April 6, 1917.

Houseflies do not have suction cups on their feet.

Houseflies cling to walls and ceilings because they have claws on the ends of their feet to cling to flat surfaces. Their feet also have hairy pads called *pulvilli* coated with a sticky substance that enables them to walk on slick surfaces, such as windows and mirrors.

{ Taxation without representation exists in the United States of America. }

Residents of Washington, D.C., pay the same federal taxes as other U.S. citizens. However, since the District of Columbia is not a state, the citizens do not elect any voting representatives to Congress, and they were not granted the right to vote in presidential elections until 1961 by the 23rd Amendment. In 1970, Congress allowed the district to elect a nonvoting delegate to the House of Representatives. In 1978, Congress passed a constitutional amendment to give the district voting representation in the House and Senate, but only fifteen of the necessary thirty-five states ratified the amendment, which expired in 1985. A majority of the district's voters supported statehood in a 1980 election and approved a state constitution in a 1982 election, but Congress never admitted Washington, D.C., as the state of New Columbia.

Never Never Land is a real place.

Never Never Land is Australian slang for the Australian outback because visitors to those vast, desolate regions vowed "never never" to return. Depicted in the 1908 book *We of the Never Never* by Mrs. Aeneas Gunn, the outback southeast of Darwin, Australia, became known as Never Never Land. *Peter Pan*, the play by James Matthew Barrie, opened in London in 1904 and followed Peter's adventures in Neverland (not Never Never Land), as do the 1911 book version (originally titled *Peter and Wendy*) and Walt Disney's 1953 animated movie *Peter Pan*. People incorrectly use the names *Neverland* and *Never Never Land* interchangeably.

{ Leap year does not occur every four years. }

February 29 is added to the calendar year only when the number of the year is divisible by 4—except in centenary years not divisible by 400. For instance, the year 2000 was a leap year, but the year 2100, while divisible by 4, will not be a leap year because it is not divisible by 400.

{ **The bagpipe did not originate
in Scotland.** }

The first bagpipe, made from reeds stuck into a goatskin bag, originated in the Middle East (probably among the Hittites) several hundred years B.C.E. The bagpipe reached Italy in the thirteenth century, England in the fourteenth century, and finally Scotland in the fifteenth century.

Key West is not the westernmost Florida key.

West of Key West are the Marquesas Keys, followed by the Dry Tortugas, home of Fort Jefferson National Monument.

Heinz does not make 57 varieties.

In 1896, while riding an elevated train in New York City, company founder H. J. Heinz spotted an advertisement for a shoe store, announcing "21 Styles" of shoes. Inspired by the concept, Heinz immediately decided to use it to advertise his pickles and condiments. Although Heinz made more than sixty different products at the time, he settled on the slogan "57 Varieties" because he liked the way it looked in print. Today, the H. J. Heinz Company makes more than 3,000 varieties, but still uses the "57 Varieties" slogan.

Abraham Lincoln did not write the Gettysburg Address on the back of an envelope while riding the train to Gettysburg.

Lincoln started writing the Gettysburg Address on Sunday, November 8, 1863, nearly two weeks before delivering the address on November 19. He wrote five drafts. He drafted the final version of the Gettysburg Address on executive letterhead and was probably finished the night before the battlefield dedication ceremony. According to Lincoln's private secretary, the president did no writing on the bumpy train ride to Gettysburg. Lincoln's speech at the dedication of the Gettysburg Cemetery lasted about two minutes.

In 1885, twenty-two years after the address, Lincoln's son Robert (a student at Harvard when his father delivered the speech in the fall of 1863) claimed in a letter that his father wrote the speech on the train.

Old Ironsides was not made from iron.

The American frigate *Constitution*, launched in 1797, was nicknamed *Old Ironsides* during the War of 1812 after some cannonballs fired by the British warship *Guerriere* bounced off its sturdy oak sides. Repaired and rebuilt several

times, *Old Ironsides* docked on the Charles River near Boston and, still in commission, remains the oldest warship afloat in any of the world's navies. The first known all-iron sailing ship was the *Vulcan*, launched by the British in 1818. The first battle between American ironclad ships took place on March 8, 1862, during the Civil War, between the *Monitor* and the *Virginia* (formerly called the *Merrimack*).

British prisoners did not settle Australia.

Australia's first settlers, the Koori people, reached the continent some 50,000 years ago—probably from Asia by way of New Guinea. In 1606 C.E., Dutch navigator Willem Jansz, convinced he had landed in New Guinea, became the first European to sight and land in Australia. In 1788, the first British settlers (approximately 730 exiled prisoners and 200 guards and their families) arrived in Botany Bay and established the first European settlement and the beginning of the city of Sydney. At the time, 300,000 Koori people lived on the continent. The British settlers considered them a primitive people, called them *Aborigines,* and confiscated their land.

{ The guillotine was not invented by Dr. Joseph Guillotin in France. }

During the French Revolution, Dr. Joseph Ignace Guillotin recommended that the French National Assembly adopt the beheading machine as the official device for all executions—to replace such inhumane methods as public hangings and quarterings. Ancient Persians purportedly had a similar beheading machine, as did the Italians in the thirteenth century and the Scots during the Middle Ages. Dr. Guillotin hoped that the decapitation machine he designed would be an interim step toward completely banning the death penalty. On April 25, 1792, the French National Assembly passed a law making decapitation the uniform method of capital punishment. France used the guillotine for executions until 1981, when the country abolished capital punishment—fulfilling Dr. Guillotin's dream and proving he was truly ahead of his time.

Napalm was not used for the first time in the Vietnam War.

In 1942, during world War II, Harvard University chemist Louis Fieser created napalm (a combination of naphthenic acid and palmitic acid). The jellied gasoline, developed in 1944 by Standard Oil and DuPont chemical companies, clings to everything it touches and burns violently. On March 9, 1945, General Curtis LeMay ordered U.S. Air Force bombers to drop nearly 2,000 tons of napalm bombs on Tokyo, killing at least 83,000 people, injuring more than 40,000, leaving up to one million homeless, and burning down as much as one-fourth of the city. America also used napalm in the Korean War.

{ The needle of a compass does not point to the North Pole. }

The North Pole is the northern tip of the Earth's axis. The needle of a compass points to the magnetic north pole (created by the Earth's magnetism), which moves over time, slowly drifting over the Canadian Arctic. The Geological Survey of Canada completed a magnetic survey in May 2001 and established that the magnetic north pole is moving approximately northwest at thirty miles per year. As of 2005, the magnetic north pole was located at 82.7 degrees north latitude by 114.4 degrees west longitude—northwest of Ellef Ringnes Island in Canada. Every day the magnetic pole wanders irregularly around this average position and may be displaced by sixty miles or more.

{ The ostrich does not bury its head in the sand. }

Ancient Arabs started this myth, and unsuspecting Roman writers perpetuated it. The ostrich does poke its head into bushes and sometimes sleeps with its head on the ground. Also, according to the San Diego Zoo, "When an ostrich senses danger and cannot run away, it flops to the ground and remains still, with its head and neck flat on the ground in front of it." The head and neck blend in with the soil, giving the appearance that its head is buried in the sand.

Delilah did not cut Samson's hair.

In the Bible, an unnamed man—not Delilah—cuts Samson's hair. Although Samson fell in love with Delilah, he refused to tell her the secret source of his strength. According to the Book of Judges, she nagged him until "his soul was vexed unto death." Finally, he revealed that his uncut hair was the secret of his strength. Then Delilah "made him sleep upon her knees; and she called for a man, and had the seven locks of his head shaven off."

The Pledge of Allegiance to the United States flag was not written in 1776.

The Pledge of Allegiance first appeared in 1892 in *Youth's Companion,* a magazine published in Boston for boys. Associate editor Francis Bellamy wrote the

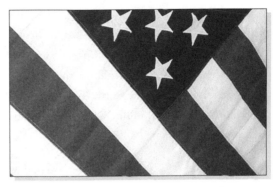

pledge in response to President Benjamin Harrison's call for patriotic exercises in schools to mark the 400th anniversary of Columbus Day. During the National School Celebration held that year, public school children first recited the pledge while saluting the flag. In 1923 and 1924, the National Flag Conferences of the American Legion expanded the original wording. In 1942, Congress added the pledge to its code for the use of the flag. In 1954, Congress added the words "under God" to the pledge.

Hank Aaron does not hold the world's record for home runs.

Although Hank Aaron batted 755 home runs during his career, Sadaharu Oh of Japan's Yomiuri Giants broke Aaron's record on September 3, 1977, and hit 868 home runs during his baseball career. Joshua Gibson, a catcher in the 1930s for the Homestead Grays and Pittsburgh Crawfords (Negro League clubs), hit an estimated 900 home runs in his career (most probably including exhibition games).

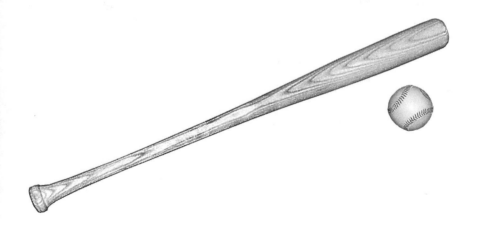

George Washington did not chop down a cherry tree as a boy.

The story first appears in the fifth edition of the book *Life and Memorable Actions of George Washington* by Parson Mason Locke Weems, published in 1806, seven years after Washington's death. Weems, well-known for inventing biographical anecdotes, did not include the cherry-tree story in the first four editions of the book and attributes it to an unidentified "excellent lady" allegedly associated with the Washington household. In the story, six-year-old George takes his hatchet and chops up the bark of a cherry tree (without chopping the tree down). The next day, his father asks the boy who killed the cherry tree. George, holding the hatchet in his hands, confesses.

Frankenstein was not a monster.

In both the 1818 novel (*Frankenstein, or the Modern Prometheus,* written by Mary Shelley at age eighteen) and the 1931 movie (*Frankenstein* starring Boris Karloff), Frankenstein is the name of Victor Frankenstein, a student of natural psychology, who *creates* the monster. In the novel, Frankenstein names his monster Adam. In the movie, the monster goes unnamed.

The British government does not own Buckingham Palace.

In 1761, King George III privately purchased the residence originally built in 1703 by John Sheffield, the Duke of Buckingham. Ownership of the building has been handed down through the royal family ever since. Today, Queen Elizabeth II privately owns Buckingham Palace, Windsor Castle, Balmoral Castle, Sandringham, Hampton Court, the Tower of London, the State coaches, the royal yacht, the royal train, the royal parks in London, and the crown jewels.

{ Abner Doubleday did not invent baseball in Cooperstown, New York. }

In 1908, sports equipment manufacturer Albert Spalding set up a three-man committee to investigate the origins of baseball. Former National League president Abraham Mills, serving as chairman of that committee, interviewed Abner Graves, who claimed that his schoolmate, Abner Doubleday, had invented the game in 1839 in Cooperstown, New York. In 1839, however, Doubleday was a West Point cadet unable to return home for the summer. Baseball is actually a slight variation on the British game of rounders (referred to as "baseball" in Jane Austen's 1798 novel *NorthangeAbbey* and described in *The Boys Own Book*, first published in London in 1828). American youngsters were playing the game, called "Base Ball" or "Goal Ball," as early as 1834. In the 1840s, New York Bank clerk Alexander Cartwright formed the Knickerbocker Base Ball Club with several friends and devised the rules of the game.

The word *booze* does not come from E. C. Booz of Philadelphia, who put his last name on the first "booze" bottle.

During the U.S. presidential campaign of 1840, a Democratic newspaper charged that all Whig party candidate William Henry Harrison wanted for the rest of his life was a pension, a log cabin, and plenty of hard cider. The Whigs turned this sneer to their advantage, promoting Harrison as "the log cabin, hard cider" candidate. The Whigs handed out bottles of "Old Cabin Whiskey" shaped like a log cabin and manufactured by a Philadelphia distiller named E. C. Booz, popularizing the word *booze*. The word *booze*, however, dates as far back as the fourteenth century and is derived from the Dutch word *buizen* ("to drink to excess"). By the sixteenth century, the word *buizing* had been adopted in English, and the British turned the infinitive of that verb into a slang noun for liquor. The word *bouzing* appears in Edmund Spenser's 1590 poem, *The Faerie Queene*, and in 1722, Benjamin Franklin published the word *boozy* as one of his 225 synonyms for "drunk."

{ Dungarees did not originate in America. }

Dungaree cloth was developed in Dungri, India, a suburb of Bombay, as early as the seventeenth century. Denim, also developed in the seventeenth century, originated in Nîmes, France. Called *serge de Nîmes* in Europe, the name of the fabric was pronounced *denim* in the United States. In the 1860s, a Jewish tailor named Levi Strauss, who had been making overalls from canvas for miners in California's gold rush, switched to denim, dyeing the fabric indigo blue to hide stains and making the sturdy pants even more popular.

The Mayflower did not land at Plymouth Rock.

The Pilgrims landed the *Mayflower* at Provincetown on Cape Cod on November 25, 1620, but deemed the spot unsuitable. Leaving the *Mayflower* anchored at Provincetown, Captain Miles Standish led a scouting party in a small open boat and landed at Eastham on December 10, Clark's Island on December 19, and Plymouth on December 21. The *Mayflower* reached Plymouth on December 26. The Pilgrims who landed in 1620 never mentioned Plymouth Rock in any of their diaries. In 1741, when the town planned to cover the granite rock with a wharf, Thomas Faunce, born twenty-six years after the landing, insisted that his father (who had arrived three years after the landing) told him the Pilgrims set foot at Plymouth using the rock as a stepping-stone. The rock broke in two when the townspeople tried to move it into town during the Revolutionary War. In 1920, to celebrate the 300th anniversary of the *Mayflower's* landing, a shrine was built to house the rock.

Dracula was a real person.

Irish author Bram Stoker named Count Dracula, his fictional vampire, after Prince Vlad IV of Walachia, the brutal tyrant who ruled the region south of the Transylvanian Alps (now part of Romania) from 1456 to 1462. During those six years, Vlad IV, the son of Vlad Dracul (Romanian for "Devil"), executed thousands of people by impaling them on pointed stakes, earning him the nicknames *Vlad Tepes* ("the Impaler") and *Vlad Dracula* ("son of the Devil"). Stoker based his 1897 novel *Dracula* on the vampire legends that probably arose in reaction to the thousands of savage executions Vlad IV committed. In the novel, Dracula is killed when a stake is driven through his heart.

Cooties
exist.

Cooties are lice—tiny, wingless, parasitic insects that live on warm-blooded animals. Three types of lice feed on humans. Head lice burrow into the scalp of humans to feed on human blood. Body lice—commonly called cooties—spread typhus fever. Crab lice attack the pelvic region, armpits, and chest. It is easy for one person to catch lice from another person. The word *cootie* is believed to be a variation on the Malay word *kutu*, meaning "a biting insect." The word *louse*, the singular form of the word *lice*, doubles as slang for "a bad person." Head lice attach their eggs—called nits—to hairs with a gummy substance. The term *nit-picking* originated from the tedious act of having to pick every nit from the head of a person infested with lice. The term *nitwit* originated from the false idea that head lice infest only poor, uneducated children.

The Hundred Years' War did not end after 100 years.

The war began on May 24, 1337, when French king Philip VI took over the English duchy of Guienne. Five months later, English king Edward III, whose mother was the sister of three French kings, formally claimed the French throne and sent troops to Normandy. The war ended 116 years later in 1453, when the French finally expelled the British from Guienne. In 1553, British troops withdrew entirely from French soil. In 1801, England officially withdrew its claim to the French throne. The war is known as the Hundred Years' War because it lasted more than 100 years.

I Buried Paul

The Beatles did not plant clues in their albums to hint that Paul McCartney was dead as a publicity stunt to boost record sales.

According to *Rolling Stone,* in September 1969 a student newspaper at the University of Illinois first proposed the theory that the Beatles had planted clues in their albums

that Paul McCartney was dead and an imposter had taken his place. On October 12, 1969, disk jockey Russ Gibb of WKNR-FM in Detroit, Michigan, received a phone call from a listener, Tom Zarski, who told him that John Lennon mutters "I buried Paul" at the end of "Strawberry Fields Forever" and that "Revolution 9" played backward yields the message "turn me on, dead man." Gibb shared this information with his listeners, who helped him find other clues. Two days later, in a review of *Abbey Road* in *The Michigan Daily*, Fred LaBour, an undergraduate at the University of Michigan, shared the evidence with readers. As the rumor spread across the country, Beatles record sales soared. *Life* magazine tracked down Paul McCartney at his farm in Scotland and featured him on its cover on November 7, 1969, revealing the alleged clues. In 1970, when asked if the Beatles had put clues in their albums suggesting that McCartney was dead, John Lennon told *Rolling Stone*: "No, that was bullshit. The whole thing was made up. We wouldn't do anything like that."

CLUE: John Lennon says "I buried Paul" at the end of "Strawberry Fields Forever."

In *The Beatles in Their Own Words*, Paul McCartney states: "That wasn't 'I buried Paul' at all, that was John saying 'cranberry sauce.' "

CLUE: On the cover of *Sgt. Peppers Lonely Hearts Club Band,* the hand over Paul's head signifies death.

The hand over Paul's head belongs to English comic Issy Bonn, who sang the hit song "My Yiddishe Mama." "In the photograph he was waving to his fans," explained artist Peter Blake, hired by the Beatles to design the cover. "And it was pure chance that it was over Paul's head. On the other photographs we took, it's quite different."

CLUE: On the cover of the *Sgt. Pepper* album, the yellow flowers form the shape of Paul's left-handed bass guitar and spell out "Paul?"

In the liner notes to the compact disc, cover artist Peter Blake writes: "The boy who delivered the floral display

asked if he could contribute by making a guitar out of hyacinths." The yellow flowers in the shape of a generic guitar spell out "Paul?" only by a stretch of the imagination.

CLUE: The photograph inside the *Sgt. Pepper* album depicts Paul McCartney wearing a patch that reads "O.P.D," British police jargon for "Officially Pronounced Dead."

The patch actually reads O.P.P. (Ontario Provincial Police), but a fold in the patch makes the second P look like a D.

CLUE: On the back cover of the *Sgt. Pepper* album, the fact that Paul's back is turned and he appears taller than the other Beatles (which he was not) indi-

**cates that he was dead and had
been replaced by an imposter.**

McCartney appears taller because he is standing in the
foreground. His back is turned because the Beatles al-
ways struck unusual poses, such as the backward head
shot of George Harrison on the cover of the British version of *Hard Day's Night.*

**CLUE: In the booklet in the
Magical Mystery Tour album, the
fact that Paul wears a black
carnation, while the other
Beatles wear red carnations,
indicates that he is dead.**

Paul McCartney explained, "I was wearing a black
flower because they [the film production company] ran
out of red ones."

**CLUE: The song "Glass Onion"
on the *White Album* contains the
lyric, "Here's another clue for
you all, the walrus was Paul"; the
cover of the *Magical Mystery Tour***

album depicts the walrus dressed in black; and the song "I Am the Walrus" fades out to a reading of a death scene from Shakespeare's *King Lear* (Act 4, Scene 4).

The song "Glass Onion" mocks Beatle fans seeking hidden meaning in song lyrics, and John Lennon said, "I threw in the line—'the walrus was Paul'—just to confuse everybody a bit more. It could have been 'the Fox Terrier was Paul.' It's just a piece of poetry." On the cover of *Magical Mystery Tour*, John Lennon—not Paul McCartney—is dressed as the walrus. As for the scene from *King Lear*, Lennon told *Playboy* it was all happenstance: "There was even some live BBC radio on one track, y'know. They were reciting Shakespeare or something and I just fed whatever lines were on the radio right into the song."

CLUE: On the *White Album*, the mumbling heard between "I'm So Tired" and "Blackbird," when played backward, says "Paul is

dead man, miss him, miss him, miss him."

At the end of "I'm So Tired," John Lennon mumbles, "Listen for a second, monsieur, how about another one?"—which, when played backward, sounds like gibberish.

CLUE: When played backward, the repeated words "Number nine, number nine, number nine" on "Revolution 9" become "turn me on, dead man, turn me on dead man."

In 1980, John Lennon told *Playboy*: "We were cutting up classical music and making different-size loops, and then I got an engineer tape  on which some test engineer was saying 'Number nine, number nine, number nine.' When played backward, the words sound more like 'turn me on dedmun,' simply a strange coincidence."

**CLUE: The cover of the *Abbey
Road* album depicts the Beatles
walking to a cemetery with John
Lennon dressed as the minister,
Ringo Starr as the undertaker,
George Harrison as the grave
digger, and Paul McCartney as
the barefoot corpse—as corpses
in many societies are often buried.**

The Beatles are leaving EMI studios near Sir John's
Wood in London, nowhere near a cemetery. Photographer Ian Macmillan insisted that each Beatle was wearing his typical clothes, and because it was a warm day,
McCartney took off his shoes.

**On the cover of the *Abbey Road*
album, the license plate on a
parked Volkswagen Beetle reads
"28IF"—Paul McCartney's age if
he were still alive at the time.**

When *Abbey Road* was released in 1969, Paul McCartney
was twenty-seven years old, not twenty-eight. Photographer Ian Macmillan insisted the Volkswagen just hap-
pened to be parked there.

Millions of buffalo never roamed the United States.

Buffalo can be found in India, the Philippines, Celebes, and Africa. The animal mistakenly called a buffalo in the United States is actually the North American bison, a completely different animal. Bison have twenty-eight ribs and separate upturned horns; buffalo have twenty-six ribs and joined horns. In 1850, approximately 20 million bison roamed over the western plains of North America. European settlers nearly annihilated the bison. By 1889, only 551 bison could be found in the United States.

{ The caesarean section was not named after Julius Caesar. }

The term *caesarean section* comes from the seventh-century B.C.E. Roman *lex caesarea* ("law of incision"), which stipulated that if a woman died before delivering her child, the baby should be delivered immediately through incision. Caesarean sections on dead women—not live ones—were performed as early as the eighth century B.C.E., hundreds of years before Julius Caesar was born circa 102 B.C.E. Roman historian Pliny the Elder incorrectly assumed Caesar was named after a *caeso matris utero* (Latin for "his mother's cut womb"), but Caesar was not delivered by caesarean section. Earlier members of Caesar's family had been named Caesar, including Lucius Julius Caesar. Julius Caesar may have been named after an ancestor or for his *caesius* (Latin for "bluish gray eyes") or full head of *cesaries* ("hair").

The Battle of Bunker Hill did not take place at Bunker Hill.

The Battle of Bunker Hill, fought during the Revolutionary War, actually took place on nearby Breed's Hill in Boston. American commander William Prescott defended Bunker Hill, the highest point of the mile-long Charlestown peninsula, by fortifying nearby Breed's Hill instead. The British won the battle, driving the American Revolutionary soldiers off the hill, killing and wounding more than 400, and taking 30 prisoners. The British, however, lost 1,000 men doing so—a morale victory for the colonials.

Eating carrots does not improve your eyesight.

Carrots contain carotene, a good source of vitamin A. While a vitamin A deficiency can damage the body's epithelial tissues (inhibiting the manufacture of the retinal pigment rhodopsin and decreasing your ability to see in dim light), the body can use only a limited amount of vitamin A and flushes the excess from the system. Eating carrots will not improve your eyesight, but doing so can help prevent damage to your epithelial tissues.

The Great Wall of China is not visible from the Moon.

The Great Wall of China is visible from orbit around the Earth. However, in 1969, Astronaut Alan Bean, who walked on the Moon during the *Apollo 12* mission, reported that no trace of any man-made object is visible even a few thousand miles away from Earth, let alone some 239,000 miles away while standing on the surface of the Moon. "The only thing you can see from the moon," he wrote in a letter to a columnist for the Portland *Oregon Journal*, "is a beautiful sphere mostly white (clouds), some blue (ocean), patches of yellow (deserts) and every once in a while some green vegetation. No man-made object is visible on this scale."

{ People are not gored to death every year during the Running of the Bulls. }

Between 1924 and 2004, thirteen people were gored to death during the annual Running of the Bulls in Pamplona, Spain. That's roughly one death every six years. The half-mile run takes place every day for a week during the San Fermín fiesta in July—when young men and hordes of tourists run ahead of the bulls through the narrow streets. The Running of the Bulls, known as the Encierro, has been taking place in Pamplona since 1581 and was made internationally famous by Ernest Hemingway's 1927 novel, *The Sun Also Rises*. Every year, however, participants are gored or seriously injured during the event. In 2004 alone, sixteen people were gored and another forty people were hospitalized.

S.O.S. does not stand for "Save Our Ship."

S.O.S., the international Morse code signal for distress, does not stand for anything. The letters S.O.S. were adopted by international agreement in 1908 because they are easy to transmit. The letter *S* is transmitted as three dots. The letter *O* is transmitted as three dashes. The international signal word for a distress call by radio or telephone is "Mayday," derived from the French word *m'aider* ("help me").

Charles Lindbergh was not the first person to fly an airplane nonstop across the Atlantic Ocean.

American aviator Charles Lindbergh was the first person to fly *solo* nonstop across the Atlantic Ocean. His 1927 flight in *The Spirit of St. Louis*, from New York City to Paris, took 33 hours, 30 minutes. In 1919, eight years before Lindbergh's famous journey, two British aviators, Captain John Alcock and Lieutenant Arthur Whitten Brown, copiloted a twin-engine  Vickers Vimy nonstop from Newfoundland, Canada, to Clifden, Ireland, in 16 hours, 27 minutes. Alcock and Brown were knighted by King George V of England.

Teddy Roosevelt did not lead the Rough Riders on horses up San Juan Hill in the Spanish-American War.

Theodore Roosevelt did organize the First Regiment of U.S. Cavalry Volunteers, better known as the Rough Riders. The group had to leave most of their horses in Florida during the Spanish-American War, and Colonel Leonard Wood, on horseback, led the Rough Riders on foot in their charge up San Juan Hill in Cuba on July 1, 1898. Earlier that day, Colonel Wood's second in command, Lieutenant Colonel Roosevelt, also on horseback, led the Rough Riders' charge up Kettle Hill, which became mistaken for the Battle of San Juan Hill.

{ The pelvis is not a large bone below the waist. }

The pelvis is composed of five bones: the coccyx, the ilium, the ischium, the pubis, and the sacrum. A female's pelvis, flatter and broader than a male's pelvis, has a larger central cavity that forms part of the birth canal. Elvis Presley was known as "Elvis the Pelvis" for the provocative way he shook his hips.

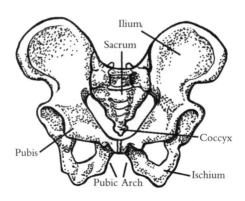

Henry David Thoreau did not live as a recluse at Walden Pond.

Henry David Thoreau, a graduate of Harvard College and Harvard Divinity School, lived in the cabin he built at Walden Pond in Massachusetts for more than two years, during which time he routinely walked to nearby Concord to chat with friends and enjoy his mother's home cooking. He also entertained visitors almost daily. Frequent guests included Ralph Waldo Emerson, Bronson Alcott, and Nathaniel Hawthorne. He chronicled his experiences in his book *Walden*.

Henry Ford did not introduce the assembly line to automobile production.

Ransom E. Olds introduced the stationary assembly line in 1902 to his Olds Motor Vehicle Company. Parts were wheeled from one workman to another to be assembled. To cut production costs, Henry Ford improved on Olds's idea, introducing the conveyor belt system in his factory in 1913.

Adolf Hitler did not create the swastika.

The swastika, a cross with the ends of the arms bent at right angles facing counterclockwise, is an ancient religious symbol of good fortune. The swastika (from the Sanskrit word *svastika*) was used on ancient Greek pottery and Mesopotamian coins, Celtic and Scandinavian artifacts, and art and religious objects from India, China, Byzantium, Egypt, and pre-Columbian America. Hitler appropriated the swastika and used its mirror image as a symbol for the Third Reich, causing the swastika to become one of the most hated symbols in the history of humanity. Since 1945, it has been illegal to display the swastika in Germany.

Greenland is
not green.

Only the coastline of Greenland is green—and only in the summer. An ice sheet averaging 1,000 feet thick covers 84 percent of Greenland, the world's largest island. (Geographers classify Australia, which is larger than Greenland, as a continent.) In 982 C.E., Norse explorer Eric the Red discovered the island and named it Greenland to make it sound more appealing to potential settlers. Greenland is neither green nor called Greenland anymore. In 1979, Greenland, a Danish colony since 1721, was granted home rule and changed its name to Kalaallit Nunaat.

Stephen Foster did not write "Way Down Upon the Swanee River" out of love for the Florida river.

The correct name of the song is "The Old Folks at Home," and Stephen Foster, who never stepped foot in Florida, wrote the song in Pittsburgh in 1851, consulting an atlas to find a melodic-sounding river name. He settled on the Suwannee River, a murky black river that starts in Georgia's Okefenokee Swamp and winds through Florida to the Gulf of Mexico. Needing a two-syllable word for the line, he changed the word *Suwannee* to *Swanee*—a river that doesn't exist. Despite the misspelling and the incorrect title, "Way Down Upon the Swanee River" is the official state song of Florida.

The Christian Sabbath has not always been on Sunday.

During the first three centuries after the death of Jesus, Christians observed the Jewish Sabbath—as Jews still do—on Saturday. At that time, Romans celebrated a day of rest on Sunday in honor of the pagan god Mithras. After the Roman emperor Constantine converted to Christianity in 312 C.E., the First Council of Nicea, held in 325, abolished the Christian observance of the Sabbath day on Saturday and created the Christian observance of the Sabbath day on Sunday—to usurp the Mithraic holiday and distance Christianity from Judaism.

Cleopatra was not Egyptian.

Cleopatra was part Macedonian, part Greek, and part Iranian. The eldest daughter of Egyptian king Ptolemy XIII, she ruled Egypt during the time of Julius Caesar and Mark Antony. Although she has been portrayed in movies by such beautiful women as Theda Bara (1917), Claudette Colbert (1934), Vivien Leigh (1945), Hedy Lamarr (1957), and Elizabeth Taylor (1960), the real Cleopatra had birdlike features— based on her portrait on coins made between 51 and 30 B.C.E.

The United States was not the first country to land on the Moon.

In 1959, ten years before the United States became the first country to land a man on the Moon, the Soviet Union launched *Luna 2*, the first unmanned space probe to crash-land on the Moon. In February 1966, the Soviet Union soft-landed *Luna 9* on the Moon and relayed the first pictures directly from the lunar surface. In June 1966, *Surveyor 1* became the first U.S. spacecraft to soft-land on the Moon.

The 1969 Woodstock concert did not take place in Woodstock, New York.

The three-day concert, originally planned for Woodstock, New York, took place more than forty-five
miles southwest of Woodstock on Max Yasgur's
farm in the town of Bethel, New York, in the
next county. The company that produced the
concert was called Woodstock Ventures, based on
the original site for the event.

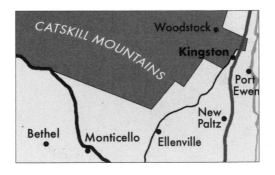

All mammals do not give birth to their young.

A mammal is defined as a warm-blooded, backboned animal with hair that feeds its young on the mother's milk. A small group of mammals known as monotremes lay eggs with a leathery shell. The only monotremes are the echidnas (five species of spiny anteaters) and the duck-billed platypus—all indigenous to Australia, New Guinea, and Tasmania.

Noah did not take two of each animal aboard the ark.

According to the biblical story in the Book of Genesis, Noah takes aboard the ark seven pairs of each clean beast, two of each unclean beast, and seven pairs of each fowl of the air. The clean beasts were those fit to be used as a sacrifice to God. The number of birds was "to keep seed alive upon the face of all the earth."

> # The U.S. Constitution does not require that all U.S. presidents be born in the United States.

The U.S. Constitution states that the president of the United States must be a natural-born citizen or a citizen at the time the Constitution was adopted on July 21, 1788, be at least thirty-five years old, and have resided within the United States for fourteen years (Article II, Section 1). Since the United States came into existence on July 4, 1776, no natural-born citizen could be elected president of the United States until July 4, 1811. The first president born in the United States was the eighth, Martin Van Buren, born December 5, 1782.

Big Ben is not the clock tower in London.

Big Ben is the name of the largest bell in the clock tower of the Houses of Parliament in London. The thirteen-ton bell, installed in 1859, was named after Sir Benjamin Hall, the commissioner of works at the time, who was tall, stout, and nicknamed Big Ben. The official name of the clock tower is the Clock Tower.

All graduating medical students do not take the Hippocratic oath.

Graduating medical students are not legally required to take the Hippocratic oath, an expression of medical ethics attributed to the ancient Greek physician Hippocrates (circa 460–370 B.C.E.). The Hippocratic oath has a doctor swear by Apollo and all the gods and goddesses to regard his teacher's children as his own siblings, to teach them medicine for free, to not give a woman an instrument to produce abortion, and not to cut a person suffering from a kidney stone. Regarded by scholars as the father of modern medicine, Hippocrates erroneously believed that air, not blood, traveled through veins and that vapors secreted from undigested foods in the body caused disease.

Eggs Benedict was not named after Benedict Arnold.

Eggs Benedict was named after socialite Samuel Benedict, who, suffering from a hangover one morning in 1894, asked the maître d'hôtel in New York City's Waldorf-Astoria Hotel for bacon and poached eggs on toast with Hollandaise sauce. The maître d' substituted ham for the bacon and an English muffin for the toast, creating a new breakfast sensation. Benedict Arnold, the most famous traitor in American history, never ate Eggs Benedict—because he died in 1801, ninety-three years before the dish was invented.

Istanbul was not originally named Constantinople.

Istanbul—the largest city in Turkey and the only major city in the world located on two continents—was founded by the Greeks in 660 B.C.E. and was originally named Byzantium. In 330 C.E., Constantine I, emperor of the Roman Empire, made Byzantium his capital and renamed the city after himself. In 1453, the Ottoman Turks conquered Constantinople, made it the capital of the Ottoman Empire, and called it Istanbul.

{ Marco Polo did not discover pasta in China and first introduce it to Italy. }

The Etruscans had pasta—made from flour and water—as early as the fourth century B.C.E. The ancient Romans, Greeks, and Egyptians knew about pasta thousands of years ago. In his 1298 book, *A Description of the World*, Polo tells how the people of China ate vermicelli and lasagna noodles—indicating that Italians were already familiar with the pastas. A 1929 issue of *The Macaroni Journal*, a trade magazine, apparently started the phony story that Marco Polo first brought pasta to Italy in 1295.

No ocean water flows into the Panama Canal.

The Panama Canal sits approximately eighty-five feet above sea level. The water in the Panama Canal is fresh water, flowing from streams and lakes into Gatún Lake, formed by a dam on the Chagres River. Fresh water flows out of the canal into the Atlantic and Pacific oceans. The Gatún Locks—a set of water-filled chambers—lift ships entering from the Atlantic Ocean. The Miraflores Locks and the Pedro Miguel Locks lift ships that enter from the Pacific Ocean.

{ Galileo Galilei did not invent the telescope. }

In 1608, Dutch optician Hans Lippershey invented the first telescope in recorded history. After hearing about Lippershey's invention, Italian astronomer Galileo Galilei built his own telescope in 1609 and pioneered its use in astronomy, discovering four of Jupiter's moons. The most powerful telescope Galileo made magnified objects only thirty-three times.

Saint Patrick was not born in Ireland.

Saint Patrick was born in Britain circa 389 C.E., then under Roman occupation, in a town he called Bannavem Taberniae. Scholars speculate that it was located in Dunbaron on the Clyde, in Cumberland near Hadrian's Wall, or at the mouth of the Severn River. Pirates captured Patrick at the age of sixteen during a raid and sold him as a slave in Ireland. He escaped after six years of servitude and, determined to convert the Irish to Christianity, studied in the monastery on the French island of Lérins, returning to Ireland in 431 C.E.

> **The entrance into San Francisco Bay is named the Golden Gate, but not because it was the gateway to the gold fields.**

Explorer John C. Frémont named the entrance into San Francisco Bay the Golden Gate in 1846, two years before James W. Marshall discovered gold at John Sutter's mill in the Sacramento Valley. Frémont named the Golden Gate after the Golden Horn, the inlet that forms the harbor for Istanbul, Turkey, because the entrance to San Francisco Bay reminded him of the harbor in Istanbul. In 1856, Frémont became the  first Republican candidate for president of the United States, but lost the election to James Buchanan. The Golden Gate Bridge, built to span the Golden Gate, was completed in 1937.

{ The Chinese did not invent the rickshaw. }

Around 1870, a western missionary living in Japan devised the rickshaw. The inventor has been identified as either the missionary W. Goble (according to C. Roper's 1895 book *Zigzag Travels*) or the Reverend Jonathan Scobie, who allegedly designed the rickshaw to have his invalid wife transported through the streets of Yokohama. The rickshaw is based on the eighteenth-century French *brouette*, a sedan chair with wheels, and the original Japanese name for the device was *jinrikisha*, a combination of the Japanese words *jin* ("man"), *riki* ("power"), and *sha* ("vehicle").

The New York blackout of November 1965 did not cause a substantial increase in the birth rate nine months later.

Records show that 13.9 percent of babies born in New York City in 1966 were born between July 27 and August 14. The percentage of babies born during that same nineteen-day span during the preceding five years ranged between 13.9 and 14.1 percent.

{ **Sound does not travel
at the speed of sound.** }

There is no such thing as the speed of sound. Sound travels at different speeds depending on the temperature and the medium it is passing through. The denser and more compressed the medium is, the faster sound travels. Under standard atmospheric conditions, sound travels at 742 miles per hour at sea level when the temperature is 32 degrees Fahrenheit. Sound travels faster at higher altitudes and at higher temperatures. Sound travels about four times faster through water than through air and about fifteen times faster through steel.

Fish can live out of water.

Lungfish breathe with gills and a lunglike organ, enabling them to breathe air. The South American and African lungfish sleep out of water for months at a time buried in the mud of dried-up riverbeds. The mudskipper,

Lungfish

found from Africa, to the East Indies, to Japan, uses its muscular fins to hop around out of water on mudflats. The walking catfish of tropical Asia moves on land by using its strong front fins and thrashing its tail, breathing with lunglike organs, and journeying overland for several days.

Mudskipper

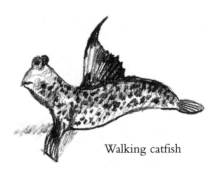

Walking catfish

{ Moses did not climb up Mount Sinai only twice. }

In the movie *The Ten Commandments*, starring Charlton Heston, Moses goes up Mount Sinai twice. In the biblical Book of Exodus, however, Moses climbs Mount Sinai at least seven times. The first time, God offers to make the Israelites a holy people. The second time, Moses tells God that the Israelites accept his offer. The third time, God instructs Moses to set bounds so the Israelites do not ascend the mountain. After God speaks the ten commandments to all the people at the base of Mount Sinai, Moses climbs the mountain a fourth time and receives the commandments that form the Book of the Covenant. The fifth time, Moses goes up for forty days and forty nights, receiving two tablets of stone written with the finger of God. After discovering the people worshipping the golden calf, Moses smashes the tablets and ascends the mountain a sixth time to atone for the people. The seventh time, he carries up two hewn tablets of stone, spending another forty days and forty nights on the mountain.

King John did not sign the Magna Carta.

King John never signed the Magna Carta, the famous document that put the King of England under the law, decisively checked royal power, and developed the idea of due process of law. Scholars debate whether the monarch could even write. He did, however, mark the document with his seal in 1215 C.E. at Runnymede.

{ George Washington never wore false teeth made from wood. }

The teeth and lower base of George Washington's dentures were carved from ivory. The upper plate was made from gold. The dentures are on display in the Smithsonian Institution's National Museum of History and Technology in Washington, D.C.

{ # The Brothers Grimm did not write Grimm's Fairy Tales. }

Jacob and Wilhelm Grimm compiled traditional fairy tales from previously published collections and by recording folklore told by peasant storytellers. The Grimms did not create any of the stories themselves. They published their collection in 1812 in Germany under the title *Kinder- und Hausmärchen* ("Tales of Home and Children" in English). The book was translated into English as *Grimm's Fairy Tales*.

Illinois is west of the Mississippi River.

The Mississippi River changed its course during a flood in 1881, leaving a piece of Randolph County in southwest Illinois, including the town of Kaskaskia, west of the Mississippi. Kaskaskia, founded in 1703, became the first capital of Illinois in 1818, but the town was destroyed when the Mississippi River changed its course. A few scattered buildings remain today.

{ Charles Darwin did not originate the theory of evolution. }

In the sixth and fifth centuries B.C.E., Greek philosophers Anaximander and Empedocles had each outlined a theory of adaptation. In the Middle Ages, German philosopher Gottfried Leibniz and English scientist Sir Isaac Newton had each suggested a theory of mutating links. In the 1700s, French naturalists Georges Buffon and Georges Baron Cuvier concluded that life on Earth had gone through a series of changes. Charles Darwin's grandfather, naturalist Erasmus Darwin, proposed a theory of evolution in his 1794 book, *Zoonomia*. In 1809, the year Charles Darwin was born, French naturalist Jean-Baptiste Lamarck formulated the first comprehensive theory of evolution. In 1858, English naturalist Alfred Russel Wallace sent Darwin a paper outlining the basic evolutionary theory, including the process of natural selection. In 1859, Darwin popularized the theory in his book, *On the Origin of Species by Means of Natural Selection*. In the book's third edition, he credits Aristotle for first coming up with the idea of natural selection.

The *Encyclopaedia Britannica* is not British.

Scottish printer Colin Macfarquhar, Scottish illustrator Andrew Bell, and Scottish scholar William Smellie began publishing the first edition of the *Encyclopaedia Britannica* in Scotland in 1768, completing the one hundred installments in 1771. The British got involved with the eleventh edition in 1910 as partners with the Americans. Sears Roebuck owned the *Encyclopaedia Britannica* from 1928 to 1943, when the University of Chicago purchased it.

Panama hats do not come from Panama.

Panama hats originated in the town of Jipijapa in Ecuador, where they are woven from the leaves of the *Carludovica palmata* tree. Few Panamanians wear Panama hats. The hats received their name during the 1800s, when Panama became a hub for shipping the hats from Ecuador to other countries. So hats off to Ecuador!

Plaque and tartar are not the same thing.

Plaque is a sticky film of mucus that harbors bacteria on teeth. The bacteria digest carbohydrates, but also produce an acid that dissolves tooth enamel, causing cavities. Brushing and flossing help remove plaque from teeth. When plaque is not removed, tartar, an incrustation composed of salivary secretions, food residue, and salts such as calcium carbonate, forms along the gum line. If the plaque and tartar are not removed, they irritate the gums, resulting in gingivitis (inflammation of the gums).

{ The French and Indian War was not fought between the French and the Indians. }

In the French and Indian War (1754–1763), the British battled against the French and Indians fighting on their side, putting an end to France's colonial ambitions in North America. England won all of France's North American territories east of the Mississippi River (except for two small islands south of Newfoundland). England persuaded France to give New Orleans and the Louisiana territory west of the Mississippi River to Spain, and in exchange, Spain gave Florida to England.

{ # West Virginia is not
west of Virginia. }

The westernmost point of West Virginia (near the city of Louisa) is fifty miles east of the westernmost point of Virginia (Cumberland Gap National Park). Most of West Virginia is actually northwest of Virginia. The two states were originally one large state, but when Virginia seceded from the Union in 1861, people living in the more mountainous regions in the western counties remained loyal to the Union, declared their independence from the rest of the state, formed their own government, and wrote their own state constitution. In 1863, Congress admitted West Virginia to the Union as the thirty-fifth state. West Virginia should more accurately be called Northwest Virginia.

Penguins do not live only in freezing cold climates.

Some penguins live in colonies near the equator on the Galápagos Islands of Fernandina and Isabela (with an average temperature between 67 and 88 degrees Fahrenheit). Other Magellanic penguins live in colonies on the temperate southwest coast of South Africa, forty-four miles east of Capetown near Stoney Point (with an average temperature between 50 and 70 degrees Fahrenheit).

And every spring, more than one million Magellanic penguins migrate from Antarctica to Punta Tombo, Argentina, to nest for six months (with an average temperature between 45 and 69 degrees Fahrenheit).

The Battle of Bennington was not fought at Bennington, Vermont.

The Battle of Bennington was fought during the Revolutionary War near Walloomsac, New York. On August 16, 1777, General John Stark and his colonial troops defeated two detachments of German dragoons that were on their way to capture supplies stored at Bennington—giving the battle its name.

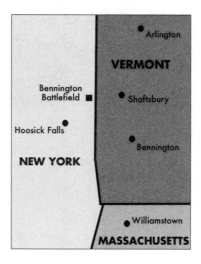

Chop suey was not invented in China.

Chop suey originated in the United States. One story contends that a Chinese cook in a California mining camp made a stew of leftovers and called it "chop suey"—a phonetic transliteration of the Cantonese phrase *tsa sui* (meaning "miscellaneous bits"). An-

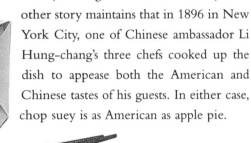

other story maintains that in 1896 in New York City, one of Chinese ambassador Li Hung-chang's three chefs cooked up the dish to appease both the American and Chinese tastes of his guests. In either case, chop suey is as American as apple pie.

Moons do not orbit
only planets.

While most moons orbit planets, asteroids also have moons. In 1994, the space probe *Galileo* discovered a moon 0.9 miles in diameter, orbiting the 32-mile-long asteroid 243 Ida. The moon was named Dactyl.

Isaiah did not predict that a virgin will give birth to the Messiah.

When the Hebrew Bible was translated into Greek in 70 C.E., the Hebrew word *almah* (meaning "young woman") was translated into the Greek word *parthenos* (meaning either "young woman" or "virgin"). Consequently, the author of the Gospel of Matthew, using a Greek Bible, misinterpreted a line from the Book of Isaiah, "a young woman shall conceive," as "the virgin shall conceive" (Isaiah 7:14). The Hebrew word for virgin is *bethulah*, which appears several times in the Hebrew Bible.

Henry Hudson did not discover the Hudson River.

In 1524, Italian explorer Giovanni da Verrazano discovered New York Harbor and first sighted the Hudson River. In 1609, English explorer Henry Hudson, searching for a northern sea route to Asia, sailed up the river to the site of present-day Albany, New York, then returned to England.

{ **John F. Kennedy was not the youngest president of the United States.** }

Theodore Roosevelt was the youngest president of the United States. He was forty-two years old on the day he was inaugurated president in 1901, upon the assassination of William McKinley. John F. Kennedy was the youngest man ever *elected* president. At his inauguration in 1961, he was forty-three years old.

Who Said It?

"Play it again, Sam."

Humphrey Bogart never says this line in any movie. In

Casablanca, Ingrid Bergman does say, "Play it, Sam," but no one in the movie ever says "Play it again, Sam." *Play It Again Sam* is the title of a 1972 Woody Allen movie spoofing *Casablanca*.

"Elementary, my dear Watson."

Sherlock Holmes never speaks these words in any of Sir

Arthur Conan Doyle's four novels or fifty-six stories about his famous detective. In the short story "The Crooked Man," first published in 1893, Holmes does reply "Elementary" to Watson. In the movies, Basil Rathbone playing Sherlock Holmes says, "Elementary, my dear Watson.".

"Ask not what your country can do for you; ask what you can do for your country."

President John F. Kennedy said this famous quote in his 1961 inaugural address, but he was not the first person to express the idea. In 1884, Oliver Wendell Holmes, Jr.,

in a speech at Keene, New Hampshire, said, "We pause to . . . recall what our country has done for each of us and to ask ourselves what we can do for our country in return." At the Republican National Convention in 1916, Warren G. Harding said: "In the great fulfillment we must have a citizenship less concerned about what the government can do for it and more anxious about what it can do for the nation." In an hortatory address in Lebanon, poet Kahlil Gibran (1883–1931) asked, "Are you a politician asking what your country can do for you, or a zealous one asking what you can do for you country?"

"It is more blessed to give than receive."

Jesus never utters this saying in any of the four gospels of the New Testament. Saint Paul, who never knew Jesus personally, attributes the saying to Jesus in Acts 20:35.

"Judy, Judy, Judy!"

Cary Grant never said these words in any movie. In the 1939 movie *Only Angels Have Wings*, he says, "Hello, Judy," "Come on, Judy," and "Now, Judy," but he never says "Judy, Judy, Judy." In the 1938 movie *Bringing Up Baby*, he does say "Susan, Susan, Susan."

"There's a sucker born every minute."

While this saying is typically attributed to P. T. Barnum, Syracuse banker David Hannum actually said it, referring to the crowds that lined up to see Barnum's replica of the Cardiff Giant, a phony fossil of a ten-foot-tall man allegedly discovered in Cardiff, New York.

"Alas, poor Yorick, I knew him well."

The line Shakespeare wrote in *Hamlet* (Act 5, Scene 1) is "Alas! poor Yorick! I knew him, Horatio."

"Go West, young man."

Although newspaper editor Horace Greeley is usually credited with coining this phrase, Greeley himself insisted that John Lane Soule had first written these words in the *Terre Haute Express* in 1851. Greeley merely reprinted the words in the *New York Tribune*.

"The only thing we have to fear is fear itself."

Franklin Roosevelt said these famous words in his 1933 inaugural address, but the idea was first expressed in the Hebrew Bible as "Be not afraid of sudden terror" (Proverbs 3:25). In 1580 C.E., Michel de Montaigne wrote in *Essays*, "The thing I fear most is fear." In 1623, Francis Bacon wrote in *De Augmentis Scientiarum*, "Nothing is terrible except fear itself." In 1831, the

Duke of Wellington told the Earl of Stanhope, "The only thing I am afraid of is fear." In 1851, Henry David Thoreau wrote in his *Journal*, "Nothing is so much to be feared as fear."

"Survival of the fittest"

Although this phrase is attributed to Charles Darwin, English philosopher Herbert Spencer actually coined it in his 1851 book, *Social Statics*.

"From each according to his abilities, to each according to his needs."

The quote does not appear in the *Communist Manifesto*, as most people think, but in Karl Marx's *Critique of the Gotha Program* as a paraphrase of a quote by Louis Blanc from *Organisation du Travail* (1840): "Let each produce according to his aptitudes and his force; let each consume according to his need."

"I disagree with what you say but will defend to the death your right to say it."

This saying, attributed to the French philosopher Voltaire, was written by E. Beatrice Hall, in her 1907

book, *Friends of Voltaire*, as a paraphrase of a quote from his *Essay on Tolerance*, "Think for yourselves and let others enjoy the privilege to do so too." The closest Voltaire came to the quote was in a letter to the Abbé A. M. DeRiche in 1770: "I detest what you write, but I would give my life to make it possible for you to continue to write."

"I regret that I have but one life to lose for my country."

American patriot Nathan Hale never said these famous last words before being hanged by the British as a spy on

September 22, 1776. Hale's last words, according to the diary of Captain Frederick Mackenzie, a British eyewitness to his execution, were: "It is the duty of every good officer to obey any orders given him

by his commander in chief." However, a similar line appears in English author Joseph Addison's 1713 play *Cato* (Act 1, Scene 4): "What pity is it that we can die but once to serve our country!"

 "If you can't stand the heat, get out of the kitchen."

Although Harry S. Truman used the expression to explain why he wasn't running for reelection for a third term in 1952, his old friend Harry Vaughan originated the saying.

"Money is the root of all evil."

"The *love* of money is the root of all evil." That's what Saint Paul wrote (First Epistle to Timothy 6:10). Paul wasn't the first to say this. Three centuries before Paul's birth, the Greek philosopher Diogenes Laërtius wrote in *Diogenes*: "The love of money is the mother of all evils."

"I'd rather be living in Philadelphia."

This phrase, reportedly inscribed on W. C. Fields's tombstone, was a joke that appeared in a 1920s *Vanity Fair* magazine. W. C. Fields's tombstone actually reads: "W. C. Fields, 1880–1946."

"Let them eat cake."

There is no evidence that Marie Antoinette ever said these words. In *Confessions*, written in 1766, Jean-Jacques Rousseau tells of an unnamed "*grande princesse*" in Grenoble "who, when she was told the peasants had no bread, replied, 'Let them eat cake.' " But the incident Rousseau describes takes place around 1740, fifteen years before the birth of Marie Antoinette. The story was attributed to Marie Antoinette to discredit her.

"Do unto others as you would have them do unto you."

Jesus did not originate the Golden Rule, although it is attributed to him in the New Testament (Matthew 7:12 and Luke 6:31). Between 551 and 479 B.C.E., Chinese

philosopher Confucius said: "Do to others as you would be done by." The Rabbinic sage Hillel (circa 70 B.C.E–10 C.E.) said, "That which is hateful to you do not do unto your neighbor."

"You dirty rat."

Although James Cagney never said this phrase in any movie, impersonators constantly use the line when imitat-

ing the star of dozens of gangster films. In the 1931 movie *Blonde Crazy*, Cagney does say, "That dirty, double-crossin' rat," and in the 1932 movie *Taxi!* he says, "Come out and take it, you yellow-bellied rat!"

"Honey, I forgot to duck."

President Ronald Reagan did say this to his wife, Nancy,

on March 31, 1981, after a would-be assassin's bullet nearly took his life. However, Reagan, a former radio sportscaster, borrowed the line from boxer Jack Dempsey, who said it to his wife, Estelle Taylor, on September 26, 1926, after losing his heavyweight crown to Gene Tunney.

> **Walt Disney did not have his dead body cryogenically frozen and stored in the tunnels under Disneyland.**

Walt Disney died from lung cancer on December 15, 1966, and was cremated two days later at Forest Lawn Cemetery in Glendale, California, where the remains were buried in the cemetery Court of Freedom, just left of the Freedom Mausoleum.

The Egyptians did not invent paper.

The Egyptians invented papyrus, made by pressing thin slices of papyrus stalks into sheets. Paper, on the other hand, is made from cellulose fibers. The first paper, invented in China in 105 C.E. by Ts'ai Lun (the emperor Ho-Ti's minister of public works), was made from the inner bark of the mulberry tree, fishnets, old rags, and waste hemp. The word *paper* is derived from the word *papyrus*. Before the advent of paper, most documents were written on parchment (made from the skin of sheep or goats) or vellum (made from the skin of calves). A single book 300 pages long would require the skins of an estimated eighteen sheep.

{ Using Coca-Cola as a douche immediately after sexual intercourse will not prevent pregnancy. }

When a man ejaculates during intercourse, his semen contains up to 500 million sperm, which immediately swim into the women's uterus to reach the egg. By the time the man can withdraw his penis from the vagina and the woman can douche with a bottle of Coca-Cola, the sperm have had ample time to penetrate and fertilize the female egg.

The Chunnel under the English Channel is not the world's longest railroad tunnel.

The Channel Tunnel, nicknamed the Chunnel, between Cheriton, England, and Fréthun, France, stretches 31 miles long, with 24 of those miles underwater. The Seikan Rail Tunnel between the Japanese islands of Honshu and Hokkaido is 33.5 miles long, with 14.5 of those miles underwater, making it the longest railroad tunnel in the world. The Chunnel, however, is the longest *underwater* railroad tunnel in the world.

The Beatles did not write the song "Lucy in the Sky with Diamonds" to form the initials LSD.

John Lennon, who wrote the song, consistently claimed throughout his life that he did not intentionally title the song with the initials LSD in mind. Lennon, who freely admitted that he had dropped acid hundreds of times, was renowned for his openness and honesty. He repeatedly insisted that the song title had been inspired by his four-year-old son, Julian, who had come home one day with a picture he had drawn at school of his classmate Lucy O'Donnell against a backdrop of exploding, multicolored stars, which he called "Lucy in the Sky with Diamonds." Lennon said he had no idea the title formed the abbreviation LSD until someone pointed it out after the song had been released.

Shooting stars are not stars shooting across the sky.

Shooting stars are meteors, bright streaks of light seen briefly in the sky. Meteors result when meteoroids, chunks of metallic or stony matter, fall from space to Earth and burn up from the friction as they plummet through the atmosphere. Meteoroids usually burn up completely before hitting the ground, but those that do reach the surface are called meteorites. An estimated 200 million meteors can been seen from Earth daily.

{ Nero did not fiddle while Rome burned. }

The violin was not developed in Italy until 1,500 years after Nero's death. According to Roman historian Tacitus, who lived during Nero's reign, when the fire started in Rome in 64 C.E., Nero was thirty-five miles away in his villa at Antium. Tacitus reported that Nero raced back to the city to help stop the fire. The emperor may have played the lyre, but definitely not the violin.

Hoover Dam does not provide all the electricity for Las Vegas.

Nevada Power, the company that supplies the electricity for Las Vegas, purchases a mere 4 percent of its energy from Hoover Dam. Nevada Power operates a fuel-burning steam plant and purchases additional power from the grid to provide the remaining 96 percent of Las Vegas's electric power. Generators at Hoover Dam supply electricity to Arizona, Nevada, and Southern California. The State of Nevada receives only 25 percent of all the electricity generated.

Pandas are not bears.

There are two types of pandas, the giant panda, which looks like a black-and-white bear, and the red panda, a much smaller animal that looks more like a raccoon. Most zoologists place both pandas in the raccoon family, Procyonidae. Although some zoologists place the giant panda in the bear family, Ursidae, others insist it should be classi- fied in a separate family all its own. Unlike a bear's, the panda's forepaw has an elongated wrist bone that provides a sixth finger, and unlike the black bear, giant pandas do not hibernate and cannot walk on their hind legs.

Adam and Eve did not eat an apple from the Tree of Knowledge in the Garden of Eden.

The Bible does not mention what fruit Adam and Eve ate. It is simply called "the fruit of the tree which is in the midst of the garden." The only fruit we know for certain is in the Garden of Eden is the fig, because Adam and Eve later cover their nakedness with fig leaves. The idea that the fruit was an apple seems to have originated with Aquila Ponticus, who translated the Hebrew Bible into Greek in the second century C.E. He mistranslated a verse from the Song of Songs, "I raised thee up under the apple tree; there thy mother brought thee forth," to "I raised thee up under the apple tree; there wast thou corrupted." Saint Jerome (circa 342–420 C.E.) translated the Greek Bible into Latin, perpetuating the error.

The United States Constitution does not give citizens the right to own guns for hunting.

The Second Amendment to the U.S. Constitution states: "A well regulated militia, being necessary to the security of a free state, the right of the people to keep and bear arms, shall not be infringed." The Constitution gives citizens the right to bear arms so they may join a "well regulated militia" whose purpose is to keep a free state secure. Congress and state governments are not prohibited from passing laws to prevent individuals from using guns for other purposes, such as hunting or jeopardizing the security of a free state.

{ **Moscow's Red Square was not named by the Communists.** }

In the Middle Ages, long before the 1905 Bolshevik revolution, Red Square was named for the Russian word *krasnaya*, meaning "red and beautiful," after the fact that the enormous plaza is paved with red bricks.

Petrified wood is not wood that has turned to stone.

Mineral-rich groundwater saturates wood buried in sediment. The minerals—typically silica, calcite, and iron compounds—dissolve the cellulose in the pores and open spaces of the wood and take its place, preserving the shape and every detail of the original wood structure. The wood has not turned into stone; the wood has been replaced by stone.

The ukulele did not originate in Hawaii.

The ukulele is actually a slight variation of the Portuguese *cavanquinho*, which evolved from a small guitar called a *machete*. In the late nineteenth century, Portuguese sailors brought the cavanquinho to the Sandwich Islands (later renamed Hawaii). The Hawaiians called the instrument the *ukulele*, from the Hawaiian words *uku* ("flea") and *lele* ("jumping"). From Hawaii, the ukulele made its way to the United States, where it became popular with flappers in the 1920s and with singer Tiny Tim in the 1960s.

{ Indira Gandhi was not the first woman democratically elected head of state. }

Indira Gandhi, the first female prime minister of India, was neither elected to office in 1966 nor the head of state. In India, the president, serving as head of state, appoints the prime minister (the leader of the political party with the most seats in Parliament) to head the government. Vigdis Finnbogadóttir, elected president of Iceland in 1980, was the first woman democratically elected head of state. Also, Indira Gandhi was not the world's first woman prime minister. That distinction goes to Sirimavo Bandaranaike, appointed prime minister of Ceylon (now called Sri Lanka) in 1960.

The Canary Islands are not named after the birds that live there.

Although canaries live on the Canary Islands, the Romans named the islands *insulae canariae* ("islands of canines") because they were inhabited by wild dogs. The English name for the islands became Canary, which later became the name for the birds that also abound on the islands. So, oddly, the name of the birds means "dogs."

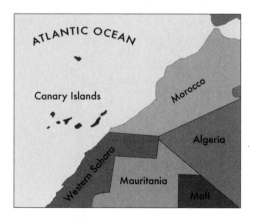

{ Hernando Cortés was not the first European to discover the Pacific Ocean. }

In his popular sonnet "On First Looking into Chapman's Homer," John Keats incorrectly claims that Hernando Cortés first looked upon the Pacific Ocean from the Isthmus of Panama. Cortés never stepped foot in Panama, although he did sail along the Pacific coast of Mexico in 1535. Spanish explorer Vasco Núñez de Balboa spotted the Pacific from the Isthmus of Panama twenty-two years earlier, on September 25, 1513. But Balboa was not the first European to spot the Pacific either. Two years earlier, in 1511, the Portuguese explorer Antonio d'Abreu sailed into the Pacific from the Indian Ocean. In 1292, Marco, Niccolo, and Maffeo Polo, who traveled by caravan across Asia to China, were the first Europeans to see the Pacific Ocean, sailing from Zaitun, China, to Singapore, via the South China Sea.

The Emancipation Proclamation did not free the slaves.

The Emancipation Proclamation, issued by President Abraham Lincoln on January 1, 1863, did not free any slaves. In the Proclamation, Lincoln declared freedom for all slaves only in areas under Confederate control. The Confederate states, having seceded from the Union, ignored Lincoln's Proclamation, which could not be legally enforced by the United States government. The Proclamation did not free slaves in Union states. It did allow slaves to fight in the army and navy, but Union slaves remained property until December 1865, when the Thirteenth Amendment was passed. The Proclamation did make the Civil War appear to be a crusade against slavery, which prompted England and France to support the North.

Strawberries are not berries.

Botanists classify the strawberry as an aggregate fruit—a fleshy fruit receptacle covered with dry, single-seeded fruits on its surface. True berries are pulpy, pitted fruits with a fleshy, soft ovary wall—like blueberries, grapes, and cranberries. The strawberry was originally called *strewberry* because the fruit appears strewn among the plant's leaves, but mispronunciation changed the name to *strawberry*.

Nicolaus Copernicus was not the first person to claim the Earth revolves around the sun.

In the third century B.C.E., Greek astronomer Aristarchus of Samos proposed that the Earth rotates on its own axis and also revolves around the Sun. Although none of his writings on the subject have survived, his contemporary, the Greek mathematician and inventor Archimedes, quoted his idea—more than 1,700 years before Copernicus postulated his theory in his book *Concerning the Revolutions of the Celestial Spheres* in 1543.

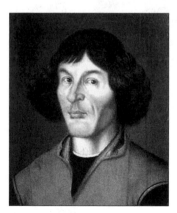

Copernicus

Mohandas Gandhi's technique of passive resistance was not inspired by Henry David Thoreau's essay "Civil Disobedience."

Gandhi first used passive resistance in 1906 in a protest against the Indian Registration Ordinance of South Africa, where he worked as a lawyer for an Indian firm. He did not read "Civil Disobedience" until 1907. Gandhi claimed that his technique of passive resistance—which he preferred to call *satyagraha* (Hindi for "soul force" or "truth force")—was inspired by the New Testament, the Bhagavad Gita, and Leo Tolstoy's 1899 novel *Resurrection*.

American Indians did not originate scalping.

In the fifth century B.C.E., Greek historian Herodotus attributed the barbaric custom of scalping an enemy to the Scythians, a nomadic tribe of southern Russia. In eleventh-century England, Godwin, Earl of Wessex, scalped his enemies. The Dutch brought this practice to America in the seventeenth century. Spanish, French, Dutch, and English colonists offered bounties for scalps of their respective enemies, and most American colonies paid settlers money for Indian scalps. In retaliation, Indians began to scalp Europeans, who then blamed them for starting the practice.

Karate did not originate in Japan.

In the fifth century B.C.E., Buddhist monks in India used a form of karate to defend themselves. In the sixth century C.E., a group called Hwarang-do practiced karate in the country of Silla, later renamed Korea. Karate developed further in Okinawa, the largest of the Ryukyu Islands, during the fifteen and sixteenth centuries. With their land occupied by a Japanese clan and prohibited from bearing arms, the Okinawans began perfecting the martial arts with the hopes of rising up against the Japanese. After Okinawa became a Japanese province in 1879, karate spread to Japan. After World War I, the Japanese began popularizing karate in the West.

{ The shortest distance between two points is not always a straight line. }

When traveling from one side of the globe to another, the shortest distance for terrestrial travel is an arc, unless you're planning to tunnel through the Earth in a straight line.

Catgut is not made of the intestines of cats.

Virtually all catgut strings are made of the intestines of sheep. Some catgut strings have been made from horse or donkey intestines. Catgut has been used for centuries to string musical instruments (and more recently tennis racquets). No one knows the origins of the name or whether catgut was ever made from the intestines of cats. Some etymologists suggest the name refers to the "caterwauling" sound created by lousy musicians on these string instruments.

Satan's name is not Lucifer.

The name *Lucifer* appears only once in the Bible: "How art thou fallen from heaven, O Lucifer, son of the morning" (Isaiah 14:12). The verse refers to an arrogant King of Babylon who intended to ascend to heaven to set his throne above the stars of God. Saint Jerome (circa 342–420 C.E.)—noting that Isaiah uses the epithet "day star," that Satan is seen to "fall like lightning from Heaven" (Luke 17:18), and that the Latin word *Lucifer* means "light-bearer"—incorrectly interpreted the verse to mean that Satan and Lucifer were one and the same. English poet John Milton popularized this misinterpretation in 1667 in his epic poem *Paradise Lost*, in which Satan is also named Lucifer.

The United States flag has not always had thirteen stripes.

The first flag of the United States, adopted by Congress on June 14, 1777, had thirteen stripes and thirteen stars, each representing the thirteen original colonies. After Vermont became the fourteenth state in 1791 and Kentucky became the fifteenth state in 1792, Congress added two more stars and two more stripes to the flag in 1795. When five more states joined the Union, Congress ruled that after July 4, 1818, the flag would revert permanently to thirteen stripes.

Mrs. O'Leary's cow did not kick over a lantern and start the great Chicago fire of 1871.

Years later, reporter Michael Ahern admitted that he made up this story to make his account of the fire more interesting. The fire did, however, start in Mrs. Patrick O'Leary's barn—but not by the cow—on the southwest side of the city on the evening of October 8, 1871. The fire, fanned by strong winds, spread north and east, raging for over twenty-four hours, killing more than 300 people, destroying downtown Chicago, and leaving some 90,000 people homeless.

Pompeii was not destroyed by molten lava from Mount Vesuvius.

In 79 C.E., noxious fumes and ashes from the eruption of Mount Vesuvius covered Pompeii. The fumes killed an estimated 2,000 people who were then covered by twenty feet of ash, which, when mixed with rainwater, hardened. In 1748, engineer Roque Joachim de Alcubierre, inspecting a tunnel for the King of Naples, rediscovered Pompeii and the plaster-covered bodies of the fleeing victims, their postures and facial expressions gruesomely preserved.

{ George Washington was not born on February 22, 1732. }

George Washington was born on February 11, 1731. Twenty years later, in 1752, England and its colonies dropped the inaccurate Julian calendar (which had fallen behind the Earth's orbit around the Sun by a year and eleven days) and adopted the more accurate Gregorian calendar. To regain the lost eleven days, the day after September 2, 1752, became September 14, 1752. To regain the lost year, New Year's Day, which had been celebrated on March 25, was moved to January 1. March 24, 1751, was followed by March 25, 1752, then December 31, 1752, was followed by January 1, 1753. George Washington continued celebrating his birthday on February 11.

Leonardo da Vinci did not paint the Mona Lisa.

Leonardo da Vinci titled the painting *La Gioconda* because the woman who posed for the portrait was the wife of Francesco del Giocondo, a merchant in Florence. According to Giorgio Vasari (1511–1574), one of da Vinci's earliest biographers, the woman was known locally as Madonna Lisa, or Mona Lisa for short. Nat King Cole's song "Mona Lisa," from the Alan Ladd film *Captain Carey U.S.A.*, reached number one on the pop charts and won an Academy Award for Best Song of the Year in 1951, helping to popularize the incorrect name for the painting.

{ Henry Ford did not invent the automobile. }

In 1769, French army captain Nicolas-Joseph Cugnot successfully operated a three-wheeled steam-powered vehicle. Around 1863, Belgian inventor Jean-Joseph-Etienne Lenoir successfully operated a gas-powered vehicle that traveled three miles per hour. In 1885, Karl Benz of Mannheim, Germany, invented a three-wheeled carriage powered by a gasoline engine. That same year, Gottlieb Daimler of Stuttgart, Germany, powered a two-wheeled motorcycle with his gasoline-powered engine. In 1888, English inventor J. K. Harley and Fred M. Kimball built the first electric car. In 1893 Charles and Frank Duryea introduced America's first gasoline-powered automobile. Three years later, Ford invented his gasoline car.

Germans are not Aryan.

Aryans were a group of people who settled in Iran and northern India (near the Caspian Sea) about 1500 B.C.E., spoke the Aryan language, and migrated west into Europe and east into India. The word *aryan* is Sanskrit for "nobles." In 1855, French count Joseph Arthur Gobineau suggested, in his controversial essay *The Inequality of the Human Races*, that the Nordic peoples, with their blond hair and blue eyes, were the rightful heirs of "Aryanism." Adolf Hitler and his propaganda machine altered the theory, claiming that the prehistoric Aryan homeland was in the heart of Europe.

> **Thanksgiving did not become a national holiday with the Pilgrims' first Thanksgiving in 1621.**

In 1827, magazine editor Sarah Josepha Hale started a campaign in the pages of *Ladies' Magazine* to set aside the fourth Thursday in November as a national holiday to observe the Pilgrim celebration. Thirty-six years later, on October 3, 1863, during the Civil War, President Abraham Lincoln, persuaded by Hale's tireless efforts, proclaimed Thanksgiving a national holiday. Hale was also the author of the children's poem "Mary Had a Little Lamb."

Dresden china is not made in Dresden, Germany.

Dresden china is made in the nearby town of Meissen, home of the oldest porcelain factory in Europe, established in 1710 by Augustus the Strong, Elector of Saxony and King of Poland. Meissen china became known as Dresden china in the 1700s. China made in Dresden by Helena Wolfsohn in the 1870s is known as Crown Dresden and is frequently confused with the china made in Meissen. The Meissen factory produces porcelain to this day.

Diamonds are not forever.

The diamond, made from pure carbon and one of the hardest substances known, sublimes at an extremely high temperature, turning from a solid directly into a gas at 3,500 degrees Celsius.

Dorothy does not wear ruby slippers in *The Wizard of Oz*.

In L. Frank Baum's classic children's book, *The Wonderful Wizard of Oz*, Dorothy wears silver shoes. Hollywood screenwriter Noel Langley changed them to ruby slippers in the script for MGM's classic 1939 movie, *The Wizard of Oz*. Also, in Baum's book, we never meet Miss Gulch, the farmhands, or Professor Marvel in Kansas; Dorothy actually goes to Oz; and she doesn't meet the Wicked Witch until she gets to the Witch's castle.

Joan of Arc was not a poor French peasant girl.

Joan of Arc or, more correctly, Jeanne d'Arc was born in 1412 in Domremy, part of the independent duchy of Bar in Lorraine, which did not join the Kingdom of France until 1776. She was an illiterate peasant girl, but she was hardly poor. Her father, agriculturist Jacques d'Arc, was one of Domremy's upstanding citizens.

The Tower of London is
not a tower.

The Tower of London is a walled fortress begun by the Normans in the eleventh century and containing the Beauchamp Tower, the Bell Tower, the Bloody Tower, the Malmsey Tower, the Wakefield Tower, and the White Tower. There is no Tower of London in the Tower of London.

{ Bulls do not charge at the color red. }

Bulls are color-blind. At bullfights, they charge at red matadors' capes not because they are provoked by the color, but because they see motion and are taunted by the darts stuck in their backs and the screams from the matadors.

In human reproduction, one sperm cannot fertilize an egg.

Hundreds of millions of sperm are needed to fertilize a human egg. Each sperm secretes an enzyme called hyaluronidase. Enormous amounts of hyaluronidase are required to dissolve the protective membrane around the unfertilized egg before one sperm can get through and fertilize it.

The Liberty Bell did not crack on July 4, 1776, while being rung to announce the Declaration of Independence.

The State House Bell, recast from the cracked Province Bell, was hung in the tower of the Pennsylvania State House in June 1753 and was rung to announce the first public reading of the Declaration of Independence on July 8, 1776. A major crack first appeared in the bell on July 8, 1835, while it was being rung for the death of Chief Justice John Marshall. In 1846, the crack was intentionally widened to reduce potential damage from vibrations when the bell was rung for Washington's birthday. In the mid-1880s, abolitionists renamed the bell the Liberty Bell, referring to liberty for slaves—and the biblical words engraved on the bell, "Proclaim Liberty throughout all the Land" (Leviticus 25:10). In 1907, a second crack appeared, extending the first crack, and the bell was retired.

Florida oranges are not naturally orange.

Ripe Florida oranges naturally range in color from slightly green to the yellow of grapefruits. To make oranges more appealing to consumers, food processors dip the late yellow crop in red dye and spray the early green crop with ethylene gas to kill the chlorophyll.

The Earth is not closest to the Sun in summer.

The Earth is closest to the Sun around January 1 and farthest from the Sun in July. The seasons are caused by the tilt of the Earth's axis, not by the Earth's distance from the Sun. The tilt of the Earth's axis gives the Northern Hemisphere the most direct sunlight (longer daylight hours) between March and September, while the Southern Hemisphere receives the most direct sunlight in the other half of the year. The more direct sunlight, the hotter the temperature. That's why when it's summer above the equator, it's winter below the equator.

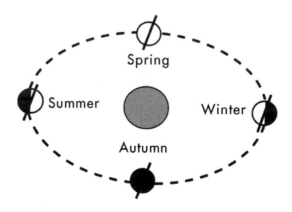

The famous photograph of American soldiers raising the U.S. flag on Iwo Jima during World War II was a reenactment.

On February 23, 1945, American soldiers raised a small American flag on Mount Suribachi, an observation post on the Japanese island of Iwo Jima. Staff Sergeant Louis Lowery, a Marine photographer, took a photograph of this first flag-raising ceremony. Several hours later, the Marines decided to replace the small flag with a much larger flag. Associated Press photographer Joe Rosenthal captured the reenactment on film, and his photograph won a Pulitzer Prize. Marine cameraman Sergeant Bill Genaust also filmed the reenactment. Unfortunately, the Japanese soon recaptured Mount Suribachi, killing many of the Marines in Rosenthal's photograph. The United States Marine Corps War Memorial, standing across the Potomac River from Washington, D.C., is based on Rosenthal's photograph.

The pope has not always been infallible.

The pope was not formally declared infallible in matters of faith and morals until 1870. That year, Pope Pius IX first pushed the doctrine of papal infallibility through the First Vatican Council. He claimed that when the pope speaks *ex cathedra* (Latin for "by the virtue of his office") on matters of faith and morals, he has divine assistance as the successor of Saint Peter, based on Jesus's statement to Peter in the New Testament, "I have prayed for thee, that thy faith not fail" (Luke 22:32).

Ping-Pong is not the name of the game.

Ping-Pong is a registered trademark of a British company that makes equipment for playing table tennis, the real name of the game. In the late 1880s, English engineer James Gibb invented table tennis, originally played with balls made from champagne corks and paddles made from cigar-box lids, as a miniature, indoor version of tennis.

Marco Polo was not the first European to visit China.

Europeans had visited China long before Marco Polo, including his father, Maffeo Polo, and uncle, Niccolo Polo, who had both traveled to China in 1266 C.E., Seventeen-year-old Marco Polo began his first trip to China in 1271, accompanying his father and uncle on their second trip. Polo is best remembered as having made the trip because his 1298 book, *Description of the World* (known today as *The Travels of Marco Polo*) became the most widely read book in Europe.

Monica Lewinsky did not perform oral sex with President Bill Clinton in the Oval Office.

In 1998, Monica Lewinsky swore under oath in her testimony to a grand jury that she and President Clinton "were never physically intimate in the Oval Office." How-ever, she did testify that she had oral sex with the President in the hallway off the Oval Office, usually against the closed door to the bathroom, and in the back office.

Human hair does not continue growing after death.

After death, the human body begins to dry and shrink, revealing more of the hair shaft and giving the false impression that the hair continues growing.

Frank Zappa's father was not Mr. Green Jeans.

In his autobiography, *The Real Frank Zappa Book*, Zappa wrote: "Because I recorded a song called 'Son of Mr. Green Genes' on the *Hot Rats* album in 1969, people have believed for years that the character with that name on the *Captain Kangaroo* TV show (played by Lumpy Brannum) was my 'real' Dad. No, he was not." Zappa's father was a Greek Arab from Partinico, Sicily, who emigrated to America when he was young.

Benjamin Franklin did not invent the Franklin stove.

Benjamin Franklin invented the Pennsylvania Fireplace, a stove he thought would be more efficient by drawing smoke from the bottom rather than the top. The smoke, however, refused to defy the laws of heat convection (namely that hot air rises), making the stove inoperable. Franklin's brother Peter tried to market the stove to the public for twenty years, selling only two. In the 1790s, David R. Rittenhouse redesigned the cast-iron stove, adding an L-shaped exhaust pipe to vent out the smoke. Although he renamed the device the Rittenhouse stove, it is incorrectly known as the Franklin stove.

Adolf Hitler's real last name was not Schicklgruber.

Hitler's father, Alois, was born to an unmarried woman named Anna Schicklgruber. When Alois was five years old, his mother married a wandering miller named Johann Georg Hiedler. Hiedler signed papers saying he was Alois's father. Alois went by his mother's maiden name, Schicklgruber, until his mid-thirties, when he changed his name to Hiedler, which he spelled Hitler. With his third wife, Klara Pölzl, Alois had three children, the third named Adolf Hitler at birth in Braunau, Austria. Hitler's political opponents discovered the village scandal and called him Schicklgruber as an insult.

"Home, home on the range, where the deer and the antelope do not play."

There are no antelope in North America. The animal mistaken for an antelope is the pronghorn, which closely resembles the antelope. The pronghorn is not a true antelope and is the last surviving member of the family Antilocapridae, which evolved exclusively in North America. Antelope, indigenous to Africa and Asia, belong to the bovid family, Bovidae. Unlike true antelopes, male pronghorn have branched horns.

The Pennsylvania Dutch did not originate in Holland.

The term *Pennsylvania Dutch* results from a mispronunciation, misinterpretation, and misspelling of the German word *Deutsche*, meaning "German." The Pennsylvania Dutch are descendants of German-speaking immigrants from Germany and Switzerland who settled in Pennsylvania during the seventeenth and eighteenth centuries. The Pennsylvania Dutch comprise members of three Protestant denominations: the Amish, the Mennonites, and the Moravians.

Atlas does not hold the world on his shoulders.

Although Roman works of art and the sculpture at Rockefeller Center in New York City depict Atlas bearing the world on his shoulders, Zeus condemned the Greek Titan to hold the sky—not the Earth—on his shoulders. According to the *Theogony*, ascribed to the Greek poet Hesiod, Zeus sentenced Atlas "to bear on his back forever the cruel strength of the crushing world and the vault of the sky. Upon his shoulder the great pillar that holds apart the earth and heaven, a load not easy to be borne."

King Tut was not the wealthiest Egyptian pharaoh who ever lived.

Grave robbers emptied most of the pharaohs' tombs at Thebes centuries ago, so when British archaeologist Howard Carter discovered King Tut's tomb in 1922, the treasures inside were considered a remarkable find. However, Tutankhamen, who became pharaoh of the XVIII dynasty as a child and died at the age of eighteen, was an insignificant boy-king whose unanticipated funeral was arranged in haste. The treasures found give just a small taste of the grandeur of the artifacts stolen from the tombs of prominent pharaohs such as Seti I, Nefertiti, Queen Hatshepsut, and Ramses II.

The first feature-length all-talking motion picture was not Al Jolson's *The Jazz Singer*.

The first sound movies were made by synchronizing motion pictures to phonograph records. In 1926, Warner Brothers re-released the previously silent movie *Don Juan* with a musical soundtrack recorded by the New York Philharmonic Orchestra. *The Jazz Singer*, released by Warner Brothers in 1927 and starring Al Jolson, was basically a silent movie with poorly synchronized musical numbers and a few sentences of spoken words. Warner Brothers released the first feature-

length all-talking motion picture, *Lights of New York*, in 1928. The following year, Twentieth Century Fox released *In Old Arizona*, the first all-talking feature film with the sound directly recorded on the film.

A sea cucumber is not an ocean plant.

A sea cucumber may look like a cucumber, but it is most definitely a sea animal. The sea cucumber—a relative of sea lilies, sea urchins, and starfish—has a mouth at one end of its body, encircled by ten branching tentacles that look like leafy stems, catch food, and sweep it into the mouth. The Chinese eat dried sea cucumbers, which they call *trepang* and regard as an aphrodisiac.

The word *babble* is not derived from the Tower of Babel.

In the Hebrew Bible, mankind, then speaking one language, decides to build "a tower with its top in heaven," but God thwarts the plan by giving the people different languages so "they may not understand one another's speech" and then scattering them throughout the world (Genesis 11:4). The Bible says the city was called Babel (Hebrew for "Baby-

lon") "because the Lord did there confound the language of all the earth" (Genesis 11:9), cleverly transforming the meaning of the word *Babel* by using a play on the Hebrew word *balal* ("to confound"). The biblical tale may be based on the ruins of the Babylonian ziggurat dedicated to the god Marduk (a temple tower nearly 300 feet tall). The English word *babble* is an onomatopoeia (a word that sounds like its meaning) for the playful sounds infants make.

A ship captain cannot perform marriages at sea.

A ship captain does not have any authority to perform a wedding unless the captain is also a member of the clergy or a justice of the peace. If the wedding ceremony is performed outside U.S. territorial waters, it must be done in accordance with the local, state, or district laws where the parties live and in the presence of a U.S. diplomatic or consular official who agrees to issue the certificate and file any required reports. Otherwise, the ceremony must be repeated ashore and the local requirements fulfilled.

The Dark Side of Oz

In 1997, radio disc jockey George Taylor Morris at WZLX-FM in Boston first told listeners that if you play Pink Floyd's 1973 concept album *Dark Side of the Moon* as the soundtrack to the 1939 movie classic *The Wizard of Oz*, the lyrics and music sync up to the action with startling perfection.

For starters, the artwork on the album cover—a beam of black light and a beam of white light going through a prism and coming out as a rainbow—can be interpreted to symbolize the rainbow Dorothy sings about and the fact that the movie switches from black and white to color.

If you start the compact disc at the exact moment when the MGM lion finishes its third and final roar, the first time you'll know whether you've lined up the album and the movie successfully comes when Dorothy walks along the top of the pigpen fence. The band sings the lyric "balanced on the biggest wave." When Dorothy falls in and Zeke jumps in to save her, the band sings, "You race towards an early grave."

From then on, the coincidences seem increasingly uncanny:

- The moment the film cuts to Miss Gulch pedaling her bicycle, the album sounds the montage of alarm clock bells, which end precisely when she gets off the bicycle.
- Toto leaps through the window into Dorothy's bedroom where the Kansas girl is lamenting to the line: "Waiting for someone or something to show you the way."
- Dorothy runs away from home with Toto, as the band sings the lyric, "No one told you when to run."
- Dorothy leaves Professor Marvel to go back to the farm to the line: "Home, home again."
- The entire tornado sequence seems scored to the aptly titled "The Great Gig in the Sky," in which lilting female vocals rise and fall with Dorothy's house as it flies inside the cyclone and plummets back to Earth again.

- When the house lands and Dorothy opens the door, the movie turns to Technicolor, a cash register rings, and the album breaks into "Money," a seeming tribute to the wealth and opulence of Munchkinland.

- Glinda, the Good Witch of the North, floats down in her bubble to the line "Don't give me that do goody good bullshit."

- The Wicked Witch of the West looks for the ruby slippers on the feet of the Wicked Witch of the East as the band sings the lyric, "And who knows which is which."

- The Munchkins' dancing seems choreographed to "Us and Them."

- The aptly titled song "Brain Damage" begins just before the Scarecrow starts singing "If I Only Had a Brain." When the Scarecrow begins dancing on the grass, the band sings the line "the lunatic is on the grass." As the Scarecrow and Dorothy dance in a circle and then down a fork in the yellow brick road, the band sings the lyric, "got to keep the loonies on the path."

- As Dorothy puts her ear to the Tin Man's chest to listen for a heartbeat, the album fades out with the sound of a beating heart.

Of course, for every moment in the film where the

lyrics and music match up, there are even more spots where they do not jibe at all.

Members of Pink Floyd have flatly denied that they recorded *Dark Side of the Moon* as a secret alternate soundtrack for *The Wizard of Oz*. Producer Alan Parsons insisted that no one in the band even discussed *The Wizard of Oz* movie while they were making the album.

Scoring a soundtrack to match a film requires timing a click track and meticulously charting the precise moments when specific actions occur in the movie. Although Roger Waters, the leader of Pink Floyd at the time, refuses to comment (fueling speculation that he secretly masterminded the alternative soundtrack), he did not write all the songs. The band developed most of the music during unstructured jam sessions while on the road. David Gilmour has said the band improvised the song "On the Run" at the very last minute in the recording studio, keyboardist Rick Wright wrote the song "Great Gig in the Sky," and drummer Nick Mason wrote "Speak to Me."

Although watching *The Wizard of Oz* while playing the synced-up CD is highly entertaining, *Dark Side of the Moon* clearly has nothing to do with *The Wizard of Oz*. Quips Mason: "It was all based on *The Sound of Music*."

The Cape of Good Hope is not the southern tip of Africa.

The southern tip of Africa is Cape Agulhas—100 miles southeast of the better-known Cape of Good Hope. Discovered by Portuguese explorer Bartolomeu Dias in 1488, the Cape of Good Hope, a peninsula jutting out south of Capetown and known for its beaches, was named by King John II of Portugal in the hope that Dias had found a sea route to India. On that same expedition, Dias discovered Cape Agulhas.

Stonehenge was not built by the Druids.

Stonehenge, the ancient stone monument on Salisbury Plain in Wiltshire, England, was built during the Bronze Age and finished approximately 1500 B.C.E. The Druids arrived in Britain more than 1,000 years later, during the Iron Age, in the middle of the third century B.C.E. In the seventeenth century C.E., English antiquarian John Aubrey incorrectly insisted that the Druids built Stonehenge, spreading this preposterous idea.

Lenin's first name was not Nikolai.

Lenin's real name was Vladimir Ilyich Ulyanov. He used the pseudonym N. Lenin. The name *Lenin* may refer to the Lena River in Siberia. The initial *N.* does not stand for Nikolai, but is a traditional symbol for anonymity in Russian writing (perhaps standing for the Russian word *nyet*), hinting that the name Lenin is a pseudonym. People incorrectly assume the *N.* stands for Nikolai because Lenin's father was named Ilya *Nikolayevich* Ulyanov.

Germans did not brew the first beer.

No one knows exactly when people started brewing beer, but the earliest record of beer can be found on a Mesopotamian tablet (circa 7000 B.C.E.) inscribed with a cuneiform recipe for the "wine of the grain." Anthropologists believe Mesopotamians and Egyptians first developed the process of malting (making barley more suitable for brewing by germinating the barley grains, developing the enzymes that transform starch into fermentable sugars). Tribes of northern Europeans did not begin to migrate into what is now Germany until around 1000 B.C.E. Vikings brewed *bior* in Scandinavia, and Julius Caesar found the various tribes of the British isles drinking ale when he and his Roman legions landed. More than likely, Gaulish monks first used hops, which have a preservative and aromatic effect on beer. The word *beer* is believed to come from the Celtic word *beor*, used to describe the malt brew produced in the monasteries of North Gaul.

The Dead Sea is not a dead sea.

Although the Dead Sea is devoid of fish, it is neither dead nor a sea. As an inland body of water, the Dead Sea—located on the border of Israel and Jordan—is actually a lake, the saltiest body of water in the world (seven to eight times saltier than any ocean), and the lowest point on Earth at 1,302 feet below sea level. Brine shrimp and a few salt-tolerant microorganisms (*Halobacterium halobium* and *Dunaliella*) live in its waters. Swimmers float with ease because the high salt content creates great buoyancy.

Mikey did not die because Pop Rocks exploded in his stomach.

Pop Rocks, the fruit-flavored candy nuggets introduced by General Foods in 1975, contained trapped carbon dioxide. When placed in the mouth, the candy dissolved, releasing the carbonation, causing fizzing sensations on the tongue and mild popping sounds. Urban legend holds that the boy who played Mikey in television commercials for Life cereal swallowed Pop Rocks, washed them down with Coca-Cola, and the resulting explosion in his stomach killed him. In truth, swallowing Pop Rocks with Coca-Cola merely produces belching. John Gilchrist, the boy who played Mikey, graduated from college in 1991 and worked as an advertising-account manager for a New York radio station. Today, Pop Rocks are sold through Pop Rocks, Inc., a wholly owned U.S. affiliate of Zeta Espacial in Spain.

Abraham Lincoln was not the first and only U.S. president born in a log cabin.

The first U.S. president born in a log cabin was Andrew Jackson, followed by Zachary Taylor, Millard Fillmore, James Buchanan, Abraham Lincoln, and James Garfield—for a total of six presidents born in log cabins. The first U.S. president born in a hospital was Jimmy Carter.

{ # Niagara Falls is not the world's highest waterfall. }

The highest waterfall in the world is Angel Falls, which drops 2,648, feet off the edge of Auyan Tepuy, an enormous tabletop mountain in the highlands of southeast Venezuela. Angel Falls, twice the height of the Empire State Building and twenty times as high as Niagara Falls, is named after Jimmy Angel, a U.S. pilot who discovered them in 1935. Angel landed his G-2-W Flamingo *El Rio Caroni* on top of Auyan Tepuy in 1937, where it remained for the next forty-three years, embedded in a bog.

Sweetbread is not sweet bread.

Sweetbread is the thymus of a young calf or the pancreas of an older calf. The thymus is an internal organ that helps form white blood cells and generally disappears when the animal grows older. The pancreas is a gland that produces a digestive juice and the hormones insulin and glucagon.

Thomas Edison did not invent the light bulb.

In 1802, English chemist Sir Humphrey Davy invented an arc light by making a platinum wire glow by passing an electric current through it. In 1844, French physicist Jean Foucault developed an arc light bright enough to illuminate the Place de la Concorde in Paris. In 1845, American J. W. Starr received a patent for an experimental illumination device utilizing a vacuum tube. In 1867, Russian electrical engineer Paul Jablochkov lit up the boulevards of Paris with arc lights. In 1878, English physicist Sir Joseph Wilson Swan patented a successful carbon-filament lamp. The following year, Thomas Edison patented his carbon-filament lamp. Edison became the father of the light bulb by building local power plants to generate and distribute electricity.

Sir Lancelot was not a member of King Arthur's Round Table.

In the original twelfth-century British Celtic legends of King Arthur (*The Black Book of Carmarthen, Kilhwch and Olwen, Historia Regum Britanniae, Roman de Brut*, and *Brut*), there is no mention of Lancelot. He first appears as a character in a French story written about 1180 C.E. by Chrétien de Troyes. In the fourteenth-century British poem "Le Morte Arthur," Lancelot became a knight of the Round Table and Queen Guinevere's lover. Around 1469, English writer Sir Thomas Malory elaborated on Lancelot's amorous adventures in "Le Morte d'Arthur."

John Harvard did not found Harvard University.

In 1636, the General Court of Massachusetts ordered that a school be established at Newetowne, later renamed Cambridge, after Cambridge University in England, where many of the colonists had studied. In 1638, John Harvard, a young Puritan minister from Charlestown, died of tuberculosis, leaving half his estate and his collection of more than 400 books to the school, prompting the court to rename the new college after him.

The tulip did not originate in Holland.

The tulip is indigenous to Asia and northern Africa and was first cultivated in the eastern Mediterranean. The word *tulip* is derived from the Turkish word for *turban*. Around 1554, Austrian diplomat Augerius Gislenius Busbequius took tulip bulbs from a Turkish garden and brought them to Europe. A craze for tulips, called *tulipomania*, engulfed Germany and Holland from 1634 to 1637, with people buying individual tulip bulbs for up to $4,000 and investing in tulip bulbs. Although the craze ended, tulip growing remained a staple of the Dutch economy.

Icebergs are not frozen ocean water.

Icebergs are huge masses of ice that break off from glaciers or ice sheets. Icebergs are made from snow that has been compressed into ice over thousands of years by its own weight. Snow melts into fresh water—as do icebergs.

Bats are not blind and do not fly by radar.

Although most bats do not see very well, all bats can see. Some species of bats navigate by sight and see well in dim light. Most bats navigate by echolocation. They make high-frequency squeaks and use the echoes to pinpoint the direction and distance of objects in the area. Radar uses electronic waves, not sound waves.

The Bible does not forbid masturbation.

Some religious fundamentalists denounce masturbation by pointing to the story of Onan in chapter 38 of the Book of Genesis to prove that God forbids masturbation. In the story, Judah marries off his eldest son, Er, to a woman named Tamar. When Er dies, Judah tells his second son, Onan, to marry and impregnate Tamar to give his dead brother an heir, in accordance with the custom of levirate marriage. Onan realized "that the seed would not be his; and it came to pass, when he went in unto his brother's wife, that he spilled it on the ground, lest he should give seed to his brother." God slays Onan for refusing to give his dead brother an heir, not for spilling his seed.

{ **"In God We Trust" has not been the official motto of the United States since 1776.** }

The verse "My God, in Him will I trust" first appeared in the King James Bible (Psalm 91:2). In 1814, Francis Scott Key wrote the lyric "And this be our motto, 'In God is our Trust' " in the fourth stanza of "The Star-Spangled Banner." In 1864, Secretary of the Treasury Salmon P. Chase put the phrase "In God We Trust" on some U.S. coins to boost morale during the Civil War. In 1955, Congress ordered that the phrase appear on all U.S. coins and paper money. In 1956, Congress made the phrase the official U.S. national motto.

IN GOD WE TRUST

George Washington never threw a silver dollar across the Potomac River.

George Washington, born in 1732, spent his boyhood at Ferry Farm across from Fredericksburg, Virginia, on the Rappahannock River (not the Potomac) at a time when the U.S. dollar did not exist. American colonists used British currency. The dollar became the basic unit of money in the United States in 1792, and the first U.S. silver dollar coin was minted two years later—although the Spanish silver dollar was widely circulated in America throughout Washington's lifetime. If Washington had attempted to throw a U.S. silver dollar across the Potomac River from his home at Mount Vernon, he would have failed. At Mount Vernon, the river is more than a mile wide.

{ Cinderella did not wear glass slippers to the ball. }

Cinderella wore fur slippers to the ball. French writer Charles Perrault retold the ancient and international Cinderella story in his book, *Stories or Tales from Times Past, with Morals* published in 1697. Instead of giving Cinderella *pantoufles en vair* (slippers made of white squirrel fur), as told in old French versions of the story, Perrault wrote that Cinderella wore *pantoufles en verre* (slippers made of glass), confusing the two similarly pronounced words. The mistake has been passed down to this day.

The Statue of Liberty is not in New York City.

The Statue of Liberty stands in New Jersey on Bedloe's Island, renamed Liberty Island in 1956. Although the island sits in New
York Harbor, it is within Jersey City's waters. An 1834 compact
with the State of New Jersey gives the State of New York control
over the island. Sales tax charged on the island and state income
taxes paid by the families who live there go to the State of New
York. A Jersey City power company provides the power on the island.

The limerick did not originate in Limerick, Ireland.

The earliest known limerick in print is found written in Middle English in a fourteenth-century manuscript, collected by Robert and Edward Harley, the first and second earls of Oxford, and kept in the British Museum:

> The lion is wondirlich strong,
> & ful of wiles of wo;
> & wether he pleye
> orhter take his preye
> he can not do bot slo [slay].

The earliest collection of limericks appear in *The History of Sixteen Wonderful Women*, published in 1821. Edward Lear published his limericks in his *Book of Nonsense* in 1846, popularizing the form. The word *limerick* derives from a party game in which each player extemporizes a five-line verse, followed by a chorus containing the phrase, "Will you come up to Limerick?"

Kilts did not originate in Scotland.

Men wore kilts in Egypt's Old Kingdom (2700–2200 B.C.E.), on the island of Crete during the Minoan civilization (2500–1100 B.C.E.), and in Persia during the sixth century B.C.E. When the Romans occupied parts of England and Scotland from 43 C.E. to 410 C.E., they brought the *laena*, a large cloak, to the British Isles. The Scots adapted this cloak into kilts and plaids.

Witches were never burned at the stake in Salem.

During the Salem witch hunts, nineteen women and two dogs were hanged and one man was pressed to death under heavy stones. More than 150 others were imprisoned. Salem was not the only place in America where witches were put to death. Before the Salem trials began in 1692, sixteen people had been hanged as witches in New England. In 1693, the town of Salem freed the people still in jail on witchcraft charges. Within twenty years, the governor of Massachusetts cleared the victims of the witch hunts of all charges, and the colony's legislature made monetary reparations to the families.

{ Eddie Haskell was not killed in the Vietnam War. }

In 1970, actor Ken Osmond, who played Eddie Haskell on the television series *Leave It to Beaver*, joined the Los Angeles Police Department as a motorcycle traffic officer. He played shop teacher Freddie Paskell on an episode of *Happy Days* in 1983 and starred as Eddie Haskell in the 1983 television movie *Still the Beaver* and the resulting television series, *The New Leave It to Beaver*, for 105 episodes. The Vietnam War ended in 1975.

In the Battle of Little Bighorn, Indians did not ambush General George Armstrong Custer and his troops.

On June 25, 1876, George Armstrong Custer and his soldiers ambushed an encampment of Sioux and Cheyenne Indians at Little Bighorn. The Indians, led by Crazy Horse, killed Custer and approximately 210 of his men. Custer, who fought in the Civil War under the temporary ranks of brigadier general and major general, was dropped to his regular rank of captain in 1865 and promoted to lieutenant colonel in 1866. He died at Little Bighorn as a lieutenant colonel—not a general.

The entrance to the Panama Canal from the Atlantic Ocean is not east of the exit into the Pacific Ocean.

The entrance to the Panama Canal from the Atlantic Ocean is more than twenty miles west of the exit from the Panama Canal into the Pacific Ocean. From the city of Colón on the Atlantic Ocean, the Panama Canal flows south ten miles to Gatún Lake, then forty miles southeast to the Bay of Panama.

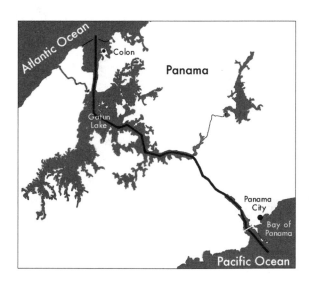

Moths do not
eat clothes.

Female moths of six species of the family Tineidae lay huge numbers of eggs on woolen and silk fabrics and on furs. The caterpillars that hatch feed on these materials, damaging clothes, carpets, and upholstery. The adult moths do not eat these materials.

{ **A drunk cannot sober up by drinking coffee or taking a shower.** }

Giving coffee to a drunk simply creates a wide-awake drunk. Having a drunk take a shower creates a wet drunk. Unprocessed alcohol in the bloodstream creates inebriation, and nothing helps speed up the body's ability to flush the intoxicant from the system.

"The Spirit of '76" was not painted during the American Revolution.

Around 1875, some ninety-two years after the Revolutionary War ended, artist Archibald Willard, a Civil War veteran from Wellington, Ohio, painted the famous picture of two drummers and a fife player leading American troops during the Revolutionary War. Willard first drew "The Spirit of '76" as a humorous sketch called "Yankee Doodle," showing three Civil War recruits parading in civilian clothes through their training camp, playing the fife and drums.

{ **Quaker Oats are not made by Quakers.** }

In 1887, Henry D. Seymour, one of the founders of a new American oatmeal milling company, purportedly came across an article on the Quakers in an encyclopedia and was struck by the similarity between the religious group's qualities and the image he desired for oatmeal. A second story contends that Seymour's partner, William Heston, a descendant of Quakers, was walking in Cincinnati one day and saw a picture of William Penn, the English Quaker, and was similarly struck by the parallels. In either case, the oatmeal packaged in the now-famous cardboard canister has nothing to do with the Quakers. The Quakers themselves sued the cereal company several times over the use of the name and unsuccessfully petitioned the U.S. Congress to bar trademarks with religious connotations.

{ **The temperature does not get hotter the closer you get to the equator.** }

Earth's climate varies according to many factors, including latitude, topography, winds, and ocean currents. Quito, Ecuador, lying almost exactly on the equator, averages 25 degrees Fahrenheit because the city sits 9,350 feet above sea level in the Andes Mountains. Nearby Mount Antisana, rising 18,717 feet, is covered with snow year round. Similarly, Africa's Mount Kenya, near the equator and rising 17,058 feet, is capped with a permanent glacier. The Gulf Stream, flowing around the southern and western coasts of Iceland, near the Arctic Circle, keeps the ports free from ice all year long. Palm trees grow in Cornwall, England—some 3,500 miles north of the equator. The warm waters of the Agulhas Current create a temperate climate along the coast of South Africa.

The Mason-Dixon Line was not drawn during the Civil War to divide the South from the North.

Between 1763 and 1767, English surveyors Charles Mason and Jeremiah Dixon determined the line to settle a boundary dispute between the Calvert family, proprietors of Maryland, and the Penn family, proprietors of Pennsylvania. The two families had battled for nearly 100 years over who was entitled to collect taxes in the disputed area. In 1820, the Missouri Compromise divided the land west of the Mississippi River and across the line of 36°30' north latitude into free states and slave states. People inaccurately used the term *Mason-Dixon Line* to refer to the border between the free states and slave states extending from the border between Pennsylvania and Maryland, along the Ohio River to the Mississippi River, and along the borderline created by the Missouri Compromise.

Three kings did not visit baby Jesus in the manger.

The Gospel of Matthew in the New Testament simply states "some wise men came from the east to Jerusalem," without specifying the number of wise men or whether any of them were kings. The wise men follow the star to "a house"—not the manger—in Bethlehem and visit the baby Jesus. (According to the Gospel of Luke, shepherds, summoned by an angel, find Joseph, Mary, and the newborn baby in the manger.) Around the third century C.E., African church father Tertullian called the wise men *fere regis* (Latin for "almost kings"). Christian scholar Origen (circa 185–253 C.E.) first suggested that there were three wise men, perhaps based on the fact that the Gospel of Matthew mentions three gifts—gold, frankincense, and myrrh. The obscure collection *Excerpta Latina Barberi*, written in the sixth century C.E., includes the first mention of the names of the three visitors: Gaspar, Melchior, and Balthasar.

{ Christopher Columbus was not the first person to claim the Earth is round. }

Columbus was not trying to prove the world was round. Educated people knew the world is round. In the sixth century B.C.E., Greek mathematician Pythagoras proposed that the world was round. During the third century B.C.E., Greek astronomer Aristarchus claimed that the Earth and all the planets revolved around the sun. In 150 B.C.E., Greek astronomer Hipparchus estimated that the Earth's circumference is 21,420 miles—remarkably close to the nearly 24,900 miles it measures. Greek geographer Stabo (circa 64 B.C.E.–24 C.E.) agreed that the world was round. Around 150 C.E., Greek astronomer Ptolemy proved that the world is round based on the round shadow of the Earth on the Moon during a lunar eclipse and the fact that the mast of a ship approaching from the sea is visible before the hull. In the Jerusalem Talmud (written between 200 C.E. and 425 C.E.), Jewish sages wrote: "The world is shaped like a ball" (Avodah Zorah 3:1).

{ United States presidents have been impeached. }

Andrew Johnson and Bill Clinton were both impeached. Impeachment is when the House of Representatives brings charges against the president. The Senate then tries the case and votes on conviction. In 1868, the House voted 126 to 47 to impeach Andrew Johnson. In the Senate, he escaped conviction by one vote.

 In 1998, the House Judiciary Committee recommended five articles of impeachment against Bill Clinton. The House voted 228 to 206 to impeach Clinton on the first article and 221 to 212 to impeach him on the second article. In 1999, the Senate voted 55 to 45 against conviction on the first count and 50 to 50 (seventeen votes short of the necessary two-thirds majority) on the second count. President Richard Nixon was not impeached. He resigned from office after the House Judiciary Committee recommended three articles of impeachment against him, but before the House of Representatives began impeachment proceedings.

{ Men do not have one rib fewer than women. }

In the Bible, God creates Eve from one of Adam's ribs (Genesis 2:21–22). Yet men and women have the same number of ribs—twenty-four each. Writes Rabbi Joseph Telushkin in *Biblical Literacy*: "The fact that every new creature depicted in the divine creation is more highly developed than the one that preceded it might indicate that woman, who is last to be created, represents the apex of creation." The Bible stresses that both man and woman were created in God's spiritual image. Woman is created from man's rib as an allegory to explain the physical, emotional, and intellectual attachment between husband and wife: "Therefore shall a man leave his father and his mother, and shall cleave unto his wife, and they shall be one flesh" (Genesis 2:24).

{ Humphrey Bogart was not the model for the drawing of the Gerber baby. }

Although Humphrey Bogart's mother was a commercial artist, Gerber baby foods were not introduced until 1928, when Bogart was twenty-nine years old. His mother may have sold an illustration of him as a baby in the early 1900s for some other product. In 1928, the Gerber company invited a number of artists to submit illustrations for its first advertising campaign. Artist Dorothy Hope Smith submitted a small, unfinished charcoal sketch of Ann Turner, a neighbor's baby. Gerber adopted the unfinished sketch as its official trademark in 1931. Turner grew up, married James E. Cook, raised four children, taught high school English, and, after serving as chairperson of the English department at a Florida high school, retired in 1990. The original charcoal sketch of the Gerber Baby is kept under glass in the company vault.

In 1896, Samuel Pierpont Langley flew an unmanned airplane weighing twenty-six pounds and measuring sixteen feet long some three-quarters of a mile along the shores of the Potomac River. The flight, lasting nearly one and a half minutes, proved that powered flight is possible. Seven years later, the Wright brothers flew the first manned flight at Kitty Hawk, North Carolina.

{ Adolf Hitler was not a vegetarian. }

In the early 1930s, Adolf Hitler began experiencing sharp cramps in his abdomen during or shortly after a meal. The pain might dissipate within a few hours, incapacitate him for days, cause days of nagging soreness, or disappear for weeks. Refusing to submit to the necessary examinations for his abdominal pain, Hitler experimented with his diet, eliminating troublesome foods by trial and error until he was down to vegetables, cereal, honey, curds, and yogurt—making him appear to be a vegetarian. In truth, he was foolishly trying to cure himself.

The "Star-Spangled Banner" has not been the U.S. national anthem since 1776.

Francis Scott Key, a lawyer from Washington, D.C., being detained by the British during the 1814 siege of Fort McHenry in Baltimore, wrote the four-verse poem, originally titled "The Defense of Fort McHenry," after seeing an American flag of fifteen stars and stripes still flying after a night of cannon fire. After his release, Key had his poem distributed throughout Baltimore. Key penned the poem to the tune of the popular British melody "To Anacreon in Heaven" (a convivial song of the Anacreon Society of London, published in 1771 and composed by John Stafford Smith to accompany lyrics by Ralph Tomlinson). Anacreon, a sixth-century B.C.E. Greek poet, wrote lyrical verses about love and wine. On March 3, 1931, President Herbert Hoover officially proclaimed the song the national anthem.

A hogshead is not the head of a hog.

A hogshead is a unit of measuring volume. In the United States, a hogshead is commonly 63 gallons, but it can be as much as 140 gallons. A barrel that holds a hogshead is also called a hogshead. The head of a hog is called a hog's head.

{ Not all Catholic priests are celibate. }

In 325 C.E., the Council of Nicea first prohibited priests to marry after ordination—meaning a priest who was already married was still permitted to have sex with his wife. In the fifth century, the Western Church demanded celibacy of all priests. Finally, in 1920, Pope Benedict XV became the first pope to prohibit priests from marrying. Catholic priests of many Eastern Orthodox Churches may be married before they are ordained. Western Catholic priests may also be married under special circumstances, such as when a married Anglican priest converts to Catholicism and becomes a Catholic priest. Peter, considered the first pope by the church, was married, as were other apostles.

Christians were never thrown to the lions in Rome's Colosseum.

Christians were thrown to the lions in the Circus Maximus, which could accommodate between 250,000 to 350,000 spectators, during Emperor Nero's reign (54–68 C.E.), according to Roman historian Tacitus. The Colosseum, completed in 80 C.E., held between 40,000 to 50,000 people and was used for gladiator battles, mock naval battles, and other spectacles. In the eighteenth century C.E., Pope Benedict XIV consecrated the Colosseum to Jesus—in commemoration of the Christians allegedly killed there—to stop the Romans from using any more stones from the Colosseum to build new buildings.

"Here Comes the Bride" was not written for weddings.

In 1848, Richard Wagner wrote the "Bridal Chorus" for a bedroom scene for his opera *Lohengrin*, produced in 1850. In the scene, servants undress a newly married couple, Elsa and Lohengrin, while a chorus sings the majestic march. In 1858, Princess Victoria of England, the eldest daughter of Queen Victoria, selected Wagner's "Bridal Chorus" as the music for her walk down the aisle to marry Prince Frederick William of Prussia. Soon after, British brides began copying the royal couple, creating a new tradition.

Koala bears are
not bears.

Koalas are marsupials—like kangaroos, bandicoots, and wombats. Female koalas give birth to tiny, poorly developed offspring. The young koalas are carried in a pouch on the mother's belly for the first six months. For the next six months, the cub rides on its mother's back.

Adam and Eve had other children besides Cain and Abel.

In the Bible, Cain kills his brother Abel, leaving only a murderer to populate the Earth. After God banishes Cain to the land of Nod, Adam and Eve give birth to a third son, Seth (Genesis 4:25–26). Adam lives another 800 years and, according to Genesis 5:4, "begot sons and daughters," but not necessarily with

Eve. Cain takes a wife (whose existence in the land of Nod is never explained) and has descendants including a musician, a metalsmith, and the killer Lamech (Genesis 4:17–22). Through Seth come "the generations of Adam," continuing the Bible story.

You have the right to make more than one phone call.

The Fifth Amendment to the U.S. Constitution gives a person accused of a crime the right to "due process of law." The Sixth Amendment gives the accused "the right to a speedy and public trial" and "the assistance of counsel for his defense." The Eighth Amendment prohibits "cruel and unusual punishments." Taken together, this means if you are arrested, accused of committing a crime, and questioned by the police while in custody, you have the right to remain silent until you talk with an attorney. If the police wish to continue questioning you, you are entitled to make as many phone calls as are reasonably necessary to reach a lawyer, family member, or friend for assistance.

The English horn was not invented in England.

The English horn is neither English nor a horn. The wind instrument is actually an alto oboe (a double-reed pipe like the oboe and bassoon). In 1760, Italian composer Giuseppe Ferlendis of Bergamo developed the English horn, known as the *cor anglais* in Britain and Europe, from the early oboe da caccia. The word *cor* ("horn") refers to its early horn-like shape. The word *anglais* ("English") could stem from a mispronunciation of the word *angle*, from the instrument's original angled shape, but no one knows for certain.

{ Amelia Earhart did not disappear while flying alone around the world. }

Amelia Earhart—the first woman to fly solo across the Atlantic Ocean, the first person to fly solo from Hawaii to California, and the first woman to fly solo across the United States in both directions—set off on her flight to circumnavigate the world at the equator in July 1937. She disappeared in the Pacific Ocean, somewhere between New Guinea and Howland Island. In the plane with her was navigator Frederick J. Noonan.

Rice paper is not made from rice.

Rice paper is made from the pith of the rice-paper tree, a small Asiatic tree of the ginseng family with a trunk three to five inches in diameter. In China, papermakers cut the trunk into cylinders several inches in length and then use a knife to carefully pare the pith from the circumference of the cylinder to its center, creating a scroll of paper with a uniform thickness. The scroll is then unrolled and weights are placed on the resulting sheet of paper to flatten it. Papermakers also make rice paper from the stems of rice straw, often mixed with mulberry and wingceltis.

The Caspian Sea is not a sea.

The Caspian Sea, the largest inland body of water in the world, is actually a salt lake. A sea is a body of water connected to the ocean, like the Caribbean Sea, the Mediterranean Sea, and the Arabian Sea. The Caspian Sea, a body of water nearly the size of California, is surrounded by land.

John Wilkes Booth was not the lone assassin of Abraham Lincoln.

John Wilkes Booth, one of the best-known actors of the time, conspired with at least four other people to bring down the United States government by assassinating the president, vice president, and secretary of state. On April 14, 1865, as Booth shot Lincoln in the head during a performance of the the play *Our American Cousin*, at the Ford's Theater in Washington, D.C., his accomplice Lewis Paine wounded Secretary of State William Seward. Three months after the assassination, the government hanged Paine and three other conspirators: David Herold (for helping Booth escape to Virginia), George Atzerodt (for planning the murder of Vice President Andrew Johnson), and Mary Surratt (for helping the plotters plan the crimes in her boardinghouse).

Booth

Paine

Herold

Atzerodt

Surratt

{ An orange is not the best source of Vitamin C. }

The camu camu, a reddish-purple cherrylike fruit that grows on trees along rivers in the Amazon rain forest region of Peru, contains approximately 2,800 milligrams of Vitamin C per 100 grams of fruit (roughly sixty times the concentration of an orange). Scientists believe the camu camu has the highest Vitamin C content of any fruit in the world. Guava, kiwifruit, broccoli, brussels sprouts, papaya, and strawberries all have more Vitamin C than the same amount of orange.

The first shots of the Civil War were not fired at Fort Sumter.

In 1860, South Carolina seceded from the Union and prepared to seize control of federal government forts in Charleston Harbor. On January 9, 1861, a battery of Confederate soldiers on Morris Island, South Carolina, fired seventeen shots at the *Star of the West*, a Union steamship heading for Fort Sumter with supplies. Three months later, on April 12, 1861, the Confederate army fired on the South Carolina fort.

The French Foreign Legion is not a haven for criminals.

The French Foreign Legion, a unit of the French government called Légion Étrangère and consisting of volunteers between the ages of eighteen and forty, does not accept known criminals or French citizens. The number of criminals in the Legion has been exaggerated in movies and novels.

India ink does not come from India.

India ink, a mixture of lampblack (soot) and gum, originated in China. It was first called "Indian ink" by English diarist Samuel Pepys in 1665. In later centuries, English authors Horace Walpole (1717–1797) and William Makepeace Thackeray (1811–1863) perpetuated the error, making the erroneous phrase commonplace.

Dinosaurs lived on Antarctica.

Millions of years ago, the continent of Antarctica was located far north of its present location, and during the Cretaceous period (beginning 144 million B.C.E. and ending 65 million B.C.E.), Antarctica matched the climate of the present-day U.S. Pacific Northwest. In 1991, an exped-  ition led by American paleontologist William Hammer discovered dinosaur fossils belonging to at least three different theropods (including a 225-foot-long carnivorous *Cryolophosaurus* from the early Jurassic period) and an unnamed herbivorous prosauropod on Mouth Kirkpatrick, approximately 400 miles from the South Pole. The fossils dated back 200 million years. As of 2004, Hammer had found fossils from eight species of dinosaur on the frozen continent.

All fish do not
lay eggs.

Many sharks and rays, guppies, and some halfbeaks and scorpion fish bear living young. Most species of shark give birth to live young after a nine-month to two-year gestation period, with some species delivering up to sixty pups in a litter. The female guppy, able to store a male's sperm in her body for several months, bears up to fifty living young every four to six weeks.

In the Bible, a whale does not swallow Jonah.

No whale is mentioned anywhere in the Book of Jonah. Jonah tells the mariners of Joppa, who are afraid of the raging sea, to "Take me up, and cast me forth into the sea, so shall the sea be calm unto you, for I know that for my sake this great tempest is upon you" (Jonah 1:12). They reluctantly cast Jonah into the sea, the waters cease raging, and God sends "a great fish to swallow up Jonah" (Jonah 2:1). After Jonah spends three days and three nights in the belly of the great fish, the creature spits him out onto dry land. We never learn the species of the fish. Incidentally, a whale is technically a sea mammal, not a fish.

> **"Neither snow, nor rain, nor heat, nor gloom of night stays these couriers from the swift completion of their appointed rounds" is not the motto of the U.S. Postal Service.**

The U.S. Postal Service does not have an official motto. The famous saying, a paraphrase of the motto written by the Greek historian Herodotus (circa 484–425 B.C.E.), is inscribed over the entrance to the General Post Office in New York and describes Persia's mounted postal couriers of the fifth century B.C.E.

The last song the band played on the Titanic was not "Nearer, My God, to Thee."

As the *Titanic* sank on the night of April 14–15, 1912, the last song the band played, before the ship's tilt sent the musicians and their instruments tumbling, was the Episcopalian hymn "Autumn," according to Harold Bride, surviving wireless operator of the *Titanic*, in the *New York Times* of April 19, 1912. Both the 1953 and 1997 movies titled *Titanic* portray the band playing the wrong song, "Nearer, My God, to Thee."

SOURCES

Adams, Cecil. *More of the Straight Dope*. New York: Ballantine Books, 1988.

Applebaum, Irwyn. *The World According to Beaver*. New York: Bantam Books, 1984.

Augarde, Tony. *The Oxford Dictionary of Modern Quotations*. Oxford: Oxford University Press, 1991.

Ausubel, Nathan. *The Book of Jewish Knowledge*. New York: Crown, 1964.

Bartlett, John. *Familiar Quotations*, 15th ed. Edited by Emily Morison Beck. New York: Little, Brown, 1980.

Bride, Harold. "Thrilling Tale by Titanic's Surviving Wireless Man." *New York Times*, April 28, 1912.

Burnam, Tom. *More Misinformation*. New York: Lippincott & Crowell, 1980.

Burnam, Tom. *The Dictionary of Misinformation*. New York: Thomas Y. Crowell, 1975.

DeConde, Alexander. *A History of American Foreign Policy*, 2nd ed. New York: Charles Scribner's Sons, 1971.

Editors of Reader's Digest. *Reader's Digest Book of Facts*. Pleasantville, NY: Reader's Digest, 1987.

Editors of Reader's Digest. *Strange Stories, Amazing Facts*. Pleasantville, NY: Reader's Digest, 1976.

The Guinness Book of Records. New York: Bantam, 1993.

Hamilton, Edith. *Mythology*. New York: Little, Brown, 1940.

Harvey, Sir Paul, ed. *The Oxford Companion to English Literature*, 4th ed. Revised by Dorothy Engel. Oxford: Oxford University Press, 1967.

Hendrickson, Robert. *Encyclopedia of Word and Phrase Origins*. New York: Facts On File, 1997.

Hertz, Dr. J. H., ed. *The Pentateuch and Haftorahs*, 2nd ed. London: Soncino Press, 1968.

Heston, Leonard and Renate. *The Medical Casebook of Adolf Hitler*. London: William Kimber & Co., 1979.

Katz, Ephraim. *The Film Encyclopedia*. New York: Perigee, 1979.

Kuntz, Phil, ed. *The Starr Evidence*. New York: Pocket Books, 1998.

Legman, G., ed. *The Limerick*. New York: Bell, 1969.

Melton, J. Gordon. *The Vampire Book*. Detroit: Visible Ink, 1994.

Metzger, Bruce M., and Michael D. Coogan. *The Oxford Companion to the Bible*. Oxford: Oxford University Press, 1993.

Moore, Laurence. *Is Greenland Really Green?* New York: Avon, 1996.

Mullen, William. "Antarctic Fossils Shed New Light on Dinosaurs." *Chicago Tribune*, February 6, 2004.

Panati, Charles. *Panati's Extraordinary Origins of Everyday Things.* New York: Perennial, 1987.

Poundstone, William. *Big Secrets.* New York: Houghton Mifflin, 1986.

Pritchard, David, and Alan Lysaght. *The Beatles: An Oral History.* New York: Hyperion, 1998.

The Random House Dictionary of the English Language, unabridged ed. New York: Random House, 1969.

Reader's Digest Guide to Places. London: Reader's Digest, 1987.

Schaffner, Nicholas. *The Beatles Forever.* New York: McGraw-Hill, 1977.

Selders, George, comp. *The Great Thoughts.* New York: Ballantine, 1985.

[Shakespeare, William]. *The Complete Works of William Shakespeare.* London: Abbey Library, 1974.

Sheff, David, and G. Barry Golson. *The Playboy Interviews with John Lennon and Yoko Ono.* New York: Playboy Press, 1981.

Shenkman, Richard. *Legends and Lies.* New York: Morrow, 1988.

Somer, Elizabeth. *The Essential Guide to Vitamins and Minerals.* New York: HarperCollins, 1992.

Speer, Albert. *Inside the Third Reich.* New York: Macmillan, 1970.

Telushkin, Rabbi Joseph. *Biblical Literacy.* New York: Morrow, 1997.

Telushkin, Rabbi Joseph. *Jewish Literacy.* New York: Morrow, 1991.

Thoreau, Henry David. *Walden*. New York: Signet, 1960.

Tuleja, Tad. *Fabulous Fallacies*. New York: Harmony, 1982.

Wenner, Jann. *Lennon Remembers*. New York: Pocket Books, 1971.

Wilson, A. N. *The Rise and Fall of the House of Windsor*. New York: W. W. Norton, 1993.

The World Almanac 2000. New York: World Almanac, 2000.

The World Book Encyclopedia. Chicago: World Book, 1985.

Zappa, Frank, with Peter Occhiogrosso. *The Real Frank Zappa Book*. New York: Poseidon, 1989.

A C K N O W L E D G M E N T S

Grateful thanks to the artists, photographers, picture collections, and private collectors who have contributed to this book.

Page vii: White House Photo.

Page 1: Detail from portrait by Gilbert Stuart, 1796; National Portrait Gallery, Smithsonian Institution, and the Museum of Fine Arts, Boston.

Page 2: Photo copyright © 2004 by Debbie Green. Used with permission.

Page 6: Declaration of Independence.

Page 7: Detail from portrait of Napoleon, National Gallery of Art, Washington, D.C.

Page 9: Art Explosion.

Page 16: Detail from *Adoration of the Shepherds* by Giovanni Benedeto Castiglione (circa 1660), Hermitage, St. Petersburg, Russia.

Page 17: Portrait of Ferdinand Magellan, Real Academia de Bellas Artes de San Fernando, Madrid, Spain.

Page 18: Detail of oil painting by Thomas Le Clear, circa 1881, National Portrait Gallery, Smithsonian Institution.

Page 19: Portrait of Benjamin Franklin by Joseph Siffred Duplessis, circa 1785, National Portrait Gallery, Smithsonian Institution.

Page 36: Official U.S. Navy Photo.

Page 42: Detail from *Samson and Delilah* by Gustave Doré, reproduced from *The Gustave Doré Bible*, 1866.

Page 47: Art Explosion.

Page 52: Illustration from *History of the World*, edited by H. F. Helmolt (New York: Dodd, Mead and Company, 1902).

Page 55: Robert Barnes Archives.

Page 63: Art Explosion.

Page 70: Robert Barnes Archives.

Page 80: NASA.

Page 84: United States Constitution.

Page 87: Photo Copyright © 2004 by Debbie Green. Used with permission.

Page 88: Photo of Blue Mosque; Copyright © 2004 by Jeremy Wolff. Used with permission.

Page 90: Photo of Panama Canal; Copyright © 2004 by Debbie Green. Used with permission.

Page 93: Art Explosion.

Page 98: Detail from *Moses Coming Down from Mt. Sinai* by Gustave Doré, reproduced from *The Gustave Doré Bible*, 1866.

Page 99: Magna Carta. U.S. National Archives and Records Administration.

Page 103: Robert Barnes Archives.

Page 109: Photo of penguin at Punto Tumbo, Argentina; Copyright © 2004 by Debbie Green. Used with permission.

Page 112: NASA.

Page 113: Detail of *The Virgin and Child with John the Baptist* by Botticelli, Louvre, Paris.

Page 114: Drawing of Giovanni da Verrazano by G. Zocchi and engraved by F. Allegrini, 1767; Robert Barnes Archives.

Page 116: *top*, Robert Barnes Archives, 1943; *bottom*, detail of illustration by Sidney Paget for "The Boscombe Valley Mystery" by A. Conan Doyle, published in *The Strand* between July 1891 and December 1892.

Page 117: White House photo.

Page 118: Robert Barnes Archives.

Page 119: Robert Barnes Archives.

Page 120: *top*, courtesy of Franklin D. Roosevelt Presidential Library and Museum; *middle*, Robert Barnes Archives; *bottom*, Soviet propaganda poster, collection of Joey Green.

Page 121: *top*, Palais de Versailles, Versailles, France; *bottom*, detail of pastel, 1736, by Maurice Quentín de La Tour.

Page 122: *top*, Truman Presidential Museum and Library; *bottom*, detail from *Christ Blessing* (circa 1460) by Giovanni Bellini, Louvre, Paris.

Page 123: Robert Barnes Archives.

Page 124: *top*, detail of an ink portrait on silk (1600s) by Kano Tanyu, Museum of Fine Arts, Boston; *middle*, Robert Barnes Archives; *bottom*, White House.

Page 126: Copy of Egyptian funeral papyrus, 19th dynasty, artist unknown, collection of Joey and Debbie Green.

Page 130: *The Starry Night* by Vincent Van Gogh, 1889, Museum of Modern Art, New York.

Page 132: Art Explosion.

Page 133: Art Explosion.

Page 138: Photo of ukulele from the collection of Mike Stein, by Joey Green.

Page 142: Detail of oil painting by Francis Bicknell Carpenter in the Senate wing, Capitol Building, Washington, D.C.

Page 144: Portrait of Nicolaus Copernicus by anonymous artist, circa sixteenth century, town hall, Torun, Poland.

Page 145: Government of India.

Page 147: Photo of karate black belt Alexandra Bruder by Joey Green.

Page 154: Detail from *George Washington* (Lansdowne Portrait) by Gilbert Stuart, 1796, National Portrait Gallery, Smithsonian Institution.

Page 155: *La Gioconda* by Leonardo da Vinci, 1503–1506, Louvre, Paris.

Page 162: Illustration of Joan of Arc from detail of an illuminated manuscript, circa 1400s, by unknown artist; Archives Nationales, Paris.

Page 163: Art Explosion.

Page 172: Detail of an illuminated manuscript by an unknown artist, Bodleian Library, Oxford University.

Page 178: National Park Service.

Page 182: Publicity photo, *The Jazz Singer*, 1927, Robert Barnes Archives.

Page 184: *The Tower of Babel* by Gustave Doré, reproduced from *The Gustave Doré Bible*, 1866, American Museum of Natural History.

Page 192: Soviet propaganda poster; collection of Joey Green.

Page 200: *Lancelot* by Howard Pyle, reproduced from *The Lady of Shalott* by Alfred Tennyson (New York: Dodd Mead, 1881).

Page 214: Photo of George Armstrong Custer by José M. Mora, 1876.

Page 218: *Spirit of '76* by Archibald M. Willard, circa 1875; Board of Selectmen, Abbot Hall, Marblehead, Mass.

Page 219: "Quaker Oats" are a registered trademark of the Quaker Oats Company. Used with permission.

Page 222: Detail from *The Adoration of the Magi* by Ulrich Apt the Elder, Louvre, Paris.

Page 227: NASA.

Page 234: Art Explosion.

Page 235: *The Murder of Abel* by Gustave Doré, reproduced from *The Gustave Doré Bible*, 1866.

Page 238: *left and right*, Smithsonian Institution.

Page 241: *all*, Library of Congress.

Page 243: *Harper's Weekly*, January 19, 1861.

Page 248: Detail of *Jonah* by Jan Brueghel the Elder (1568–1625);
Alte Pinakothek, Munich, Germany.

All other photos, drawings, collages, maps, and cartoons by Joey Green.

ABOUT THE AUTHOR

Joey Green got Barbara Walters to make Green Slime on *The View*, got Jay Leno to shave with peanut butter on *The Tonight Show*, got Rosie O'Donnell to mousse her hair with Jell-O on *The Rosie O'Donnell Show*, and had Katie Couric drop her diamond engagement ring in a glass of Efferdent on *Today*. He has been seen polishing furniture with Spam on *Dateline NBC*, cleaning a toilet with Coca-Cola in the pages of the *New York Times*, and washing his hair with Reddi-wip in *People*. Green, a former contributing editor to *National Lampoon* and a former advertising copywriter at J. Walter Thompson, is the author of more than thirty books, including *Clean Your Clothes with Cheez Whiz, The Zen of Oz*, and *The Road to Success Is Paved with Failure*—to name just a few. A native of Miami, Florida, and a graduate of Cornell University, he wrote television commercials for Burger King and Walt Disney World, and won a Clio Award for a print ad he created for Eastman Kodak. He backpacked around the world for two years on his honeymoon, and lives in Los Angeles with his wife, Debbie, and their two daughters, Ashley and Julia.

Visit Joey Green on the Internet at
www.wackyuses.com